PORTSMOUTH POLYTECHNIC LIBRARY

AUTHOR

MACAULAY, R.

TITLE

MILTON.

ACCESSION NUMBER

7262125

LOCATION

CLASS NUMBER

820·4 MIL/MAC

To be returned by the last date stamped below, or when recalled by the Librarian.

18. JUN.

CANCELLED

12. DEC. 1990 CANCELLED

-8. DEC. 1992 CANCELLED

CANCELLED

19 APR 1993

CANCELLED

22 SEP. 1999
11. JUN. 1999

When you sign out a book, it remains your responsibility until the loan form is cancelled.

820

D0294595

MILTON

GREAT LIVES

Other volumes in preparation.

MILTON

by ROSE MACAULAY

Great Lives

PORTSMOUTH
POLYTECHNIC
LIBRARY

7262125

DUCKWORTH
3 HENRIETTA STREET
LONDON   W.C.2

First Published January 1934
Second impression February 1934

All Rights Reserved

Made *and* printed *in* Great Britain
By The Camelot Press Ltd
London *and* Southampton

CONTENTS

CHRONOLOGY

1608....Birth.

1625....Cambridge.

1625 or 6..*On the Death of a Fair Infant dying of a Cough.*

1626....*Elegia Prima.*

1628....*At a Vacation Exercise.*

1629....*Nativity Ode.*
        Elegia Quinta. In adventum veris.
        Elegia Sexta.

1630....*On May Morning.*
        O Nightingale.
        Italian Sonnets.
        Elegia Septima.
  (?) *On Shakespeare.*

1631....*How soon hath Time.*

1632....Leaving Cambridge.   Life at Horton.
  (?) *L'Allegro* and *Il Penseroso*

1632–4..*Ad Patrem.*
        On Time.
        At a Solemn Music.
        Arcades.

1634....*Comus.*

1637....*Lycidas.*

1638....Travels in Italy.
        Mansus.

1639....Return to England.
        Epitaphium Damonis.

1640....Rooms in London. Teaching.

1641–2..Anti-Prelatical Pamphlets.

1642....First Marriage.
Departure of Wife.

1643–5..Divorce Tracts.

1644....*Of Education.*
Areopagitica.

1645....Return of Wife.
Publication of Poems.

1649....*Tenure of Kings and Magistrates.*
Appointment as Secretary for Foreign
Tongues.
Eikonoklastes.

1651....*Defensio Pro Populo Anglicano.*

1652....Death of First Wife.
Total Blindness.

1654....*Defensio Secunda.*

1656....Second Marriage.

1657....Death of Second Wife.

1659....Two Tracts against Church Establish-
ment.

1660....Restoration. Milton in hiding till Act
of Indemnity.

1663....Third Marriage.

1667....Publication of *Paradise Lost.*

1670....Publication of *History of Britain.*

1671....Publication of *Paradise Regained* and
Samson Agonistes.

1673....Enlarged edition of Poems.
Last pamphlet.

1674....Publication of *Private Letters and Academic
Prolusions.* Death.

CHAPTER I

EDUCATION OF A POET

THE England which bore John Milton in 1608
was, like her distinguished son, a curious paradox,
an assembly of unresolved conflicts. Renaissance
ambition and arrogance of learning, Elizabethan
splendour of poetry and drama, prose that walked
in stiff and rich brocade, prose that floundered
and spouted like a whale in the ocean, the stately
classical tradition and a spontaneous lyric loveliness peculiarly English, medieval puritanism and
scholasticism undispelled by these, with the newer
puritanism and scholasticism of the Protestant
Reformation overlaying it like a palimpsest ; a
growing and grumbling sense of personal rights
and national liberties, a swelling of that pet
vanity of the English, political consciousness,
furious convictions expressed in mannerless controversies – these characterised both mother and
son. Born two centuries earlier, John Milton
might have passed his life a monkish scholar, in
more or less continuous trouble with the ecclesiastical authorities, perhaps not a poet, certainly not
a poet up to his full stature, for the fifteenth
century lay on poetry like a stiff blanket. He
might have been an Oxford nominalist, a translator
of the Bible, a proud and controversial prelate,
or a heretic meeting a flaming end. He could,
had he travelled abroad, have drunk at the first

springs of Renaissance learning, and become a voice crying the new scholarship in the still unwatered wilderness of his native land. A century later he might have led the Horatian poets along more precipitous peaks, and been the only Whig to talk and write Dr. Johnson down. In neither age would he have been the poet both of *Paradise Lost* and of *L'Allegro*.

Yet in the England that produced and shaped him, he was a misfit. His peculiar and characteristic brand of classicism, romanticism, puritanism, modernism, individualism, Hebraism, Hellenism, Republicanism, egoism, indignation, sensuous æstheticism, and passion for a liberty of speech and thought that had not so far been conceived but by the few, made him an arrogant, self-dedicated solitary, a superb and monstrous alien.

Of country yeoman descent, he was born in Bread Street, Cheapside, of a cultured and musical scrivener. " I will now mention," he wrote, introducing thus his favourite theme into his *Second Defence of the English People*, " who and whence I am. I was born in London, of a good family, my father a very honourable man. . . ." Young John was trained by his father to music, and it remained, with poetry, history, and political controversy, his recreation and study to the end of his life. He had, says Aubrey, " a delicate tuneable voice, and great skill." Music, even more than the intellectual pleasure of poetry, could dissolve him into ecstasies. It was to scholarship and classical literature that he was, according to his own account, closely set by his father. Neither tired eyes nor headaches daunted or retarded this diligent child. At twelve or so, he entered St. Paul's, where the learned Dr.

Alexander Gill was high master, and his son an usher. They, like Mr. Milton, inclined to the Puritan wing of the Church. Though, in the strict contemporary sense of that elastic word *Puritan*, which was applied to dissenters from, or would-be reformers of, the Church of England worship, the Miltons were not Puritan, for they belonged without demur to the Protestant Church of England. John Milton the scrivener would doubtless have resented " the odious name of Puritan " being applied to him, as did Mrs. Hutchinson, and Richard Baxter in his youth.

The Miltons found pleasure in masques and profane music as well as in graver and more religious studies. If young John wrote metrical versions of the Psalms to his father's settings at fifteen, he wrote, says Aubrey, other poetry at ten, " which might well belong to a riper age," but is fortunately not extant. We see him at the age of ten in Janssen's portrait, a fair, neat-featured, thoughtful, small boy, with close-cut auburn hair, striped doublet and beautiful lace collar, showing that his mother was not, anyhow, too Puritan to set off her child's beauty with elegant dress.

The brilliant boy must have been trained scholastically to the limits of his capacities, and beyond the limits of his health and eyesight. Besides the classical studies over which he sat up at nights, he had, by his father's desire, learnt some French, Italian, and even Hebrew, by the time he left school for Cambridge at sixteen. As to his metrical Psalms, his are no worse than those by the other practitioners of that unfortunate art. He thought them, probably, better than they were. It had been found, he remarks much later, that whatever he wrote, " in English or other tongue, prosing or verse, but chiefly this latter, the stile, by certain vital signes it had, was likely to live." This is to claim too much ; and one may infer from it and from other indications, that the pride and hope of his family, dedicated and set apart for scholarship, was accorded rather more praise and honour in youth than was good for him.

His English reading was obviously, even in boyhood, wide ; but he seems to have been, like others of his generation, particularly influenced by Spenser. Sylvester's rendering of Du Bartas' poem on the Creation even more affected his early style ; indeed, he never quite shook off Sylvester, whose influence is obvious in *Paradise Lost*. Imaginative children of any period who were given to read *The Faërie Queene*, Sylvester, and the brothers Fletcher, would fall under their spell ; but in the early seventeenth century these engaging Protestant poets were intensely typical of one aspect of the English culture of their time, with their tranquil flow of lines, their decoration of fantastic imagery, and religious-romantic themes. It must have been this poetry, together with Shakespeare, Ben Jonson, the Bible, and above all the great stories and figures of Greek and Roman history, literature and mythology, that early shaped young John Milton's imagination. He habitually mentions Orpheus, Eurydice, Hermes, Bacchus, and the other creatures of the classical world, as if they were in the next field. When, at sixteen, in 1625, he matriculated at Christ's College, Cambridge, and a few weeks later entered it as a lesser pensioner, it seems safe to assume that he started on that University curriculum that was to exasperate him so much, further advanced than most other freshmen of his time. Too far advanced, in fact, in some ways, for Cambridge ; certainly inconveniently advanced in independence of mind and belief in his own views.

That he was already a good and eloquent Latin versifier is apparent in the lines (the *Elegia Quarta*) addressed, probably in his first term, to his old tutor Thomas Young, lines both accomplished, and full of the loyal affection which Milton so amiably lavished on those of his instructors who were so fortunate as to win his esteem (the others were cast into outer darkness). His feeling for Young (later the leading author of the Smectymnuan pamphlet against the Church) may have been one important factor in his hot, though short-lived advocacy, fifteen years later, of a system so unsuitable to his rebellious temper and to his classical, humanist intellect, as was the Presbyterian Church.

Young Milton entered Christ's full of ambition, intelligence, and self-confidence, thinking he was come to an Athens beside the Cam, where he would imbibe learning, and study and debate and exchange ideas with his fellows, as he had been used with his friend Charles Diodati at St. Paul's, with whom he exchanged from time to time letters in Latin. Christ's was a considerable college, under the mastership of Dr. Bainbrigge. The Fellows included the lovable and learned Joseph Meade, and the also learned, but more Arminian, William Chappell, who became Milton's tutor, and has acquired notoriety from having treated him with " some unkindness," and, in fact, sent him down for a term ; of which more later.

The Cambridge which Milton entered was still
half medieval in spirit and curriculum. The studies
were mainly Rhetoric, Logic, Scholastic Philosophy, Latin and Greek, slight mathematics, and
astronomy. A little Roman history was included ;
no English history or literature, though this could
be studied by those who so desired. Bacon's
plea for more study of history and of natural
philosophy had not so far had much effect. It
was a Cambridge of strife and attempted reform,
educational, political, theological, and sociolo-
gical. Theologically, the university was torn between Arminianism and the old Genevan Cal-
vinism. It was while Milton was still up that
Fuller quotes someone as having remarked that
" he who in his Sermons could preach *near Popery*
and yet *no Popery*, there was your man." (By
" near Popery " Fuller and his contemporaries
meant the Laudian ceremonial which the Puritans
regarded as popish, the Latitudinarians as silly.)
Educationally, a new ferment of thought was
revolting against the scholastic curriculum, and
pleading for a more humane and liberal culture,
a war in which young Milton ardently took sides,
which probably did him no good with the authorities. Morally, the new regulation prohibiting
bedmakers " of whatever age," to enter the rooms
is significant. Undergraduates who could not
even be trusted with elderly bedmakers do certainly seem to merit some of the strictures of that
shocked and pious young gentleman, Symonds
d'Ewes of St. John's, though as he was almost
equally scandalised by licentious living, swearing,
and Sunday bowls, it would be unfair to judge
University manners by his strictures, or even by
those of George Herbert, then Public Orator.

Upon the ill behaviour of some of his fellows
Milton too had, later, a word to say ; but Milton
also was a stern judge, both of intellectual and
moral deficiencies.   He shows, in his references to
Cambridge, little sign of ever having appreciated
the stature of the many able, learned and very
individual scholars who peopled the University
in his time.   His tone is usually one of complaint,
often of contempt.

The more genial Fuller gives a different impression. Among the prominent figures that
made the Cambridge of 1625–35 the learned,
lively, amusing disputatious society it was, there
was Fuller himself, racy and anecdotal ; Andrew
Downes, the Regius Professor of Greek, " one
composed of Greek and industry " ;   George
Herbert ;   Dr. Whichcote, less Puritan than
liberal in theology ;   Collins, the Provost of
Kings, " the most fluent Latinist of our age " ;
Seth Ward, the Emmanuel mathematician ;
Jeremy Taylor (who came up three years after
Milton) ;   Tom Randolph, the Trinity poet ;
John Cleveland, the satirist and Latinist ; Duport,
afterwards Regius Professor of Greek ;   old
Laurence Chaderton, one of the Authorised
Version translators (but perhaps, as he was ninety
or so when Milton matriculated, he was no longer
a very active element in University life) ; and a
hundred other intelligent and learned gentlemen.
Cambridge can scarcely have been a bore, though
it bored Milton.   " How much was there now of
Athens in Cambridge," exclaims Fuller, referring
to the many able competitors for the Greek Pro-
fessorship vacated by Downes' death.

But Milton did not see that there was at all
much of Athens in Cambridge. He perceived

quite early that he could never be a don, and that
" the studious cloister's pale," stormed as it in-
cessantly and inevitably was by tutorial and other
distractions, was not for him.

Let us picture, then, the undergraduate of sixteen and a half, the pride and darling of his home,
the prodigious pupil of his school, so delicately
beautiful of face and form, so elegantly nice in
demeanour and habit as to be nick-named in
Cambridge, " the Lady," eager for learning, and,
feeling himself dedicated and set apart for great
things. Our knowledge of his University career
derives mainly from his own self-expression, in
poetry, in a few private letters, in his academic
orations, and in various passages in his later
writings. His five almost contemporary biographers echo one another (and himself) in
recording that he " was a very hard scholar in
the University, and performed all his exercises
there with very good Applause " ; and the only
malicious one of them (Anthony à Wood) adds
" that he was esteemed to be a virtuous and sober
person, yet not to be ignorant of his own parts."
And Milton himself, who seldom leaves us in the
dark about his past, but could be stung by every
slanderer and assailant into self-exaltation and
counter-attack, tells us that he passed his seven
years " aloof from vice, and approved by all the
good."

But even this admirable University career was
not all smoothness. Milton was used to make his
own troubles and enemies as he went along, and
Cambridge University seems to have stood, from
the first, somewhat in the north of his favour.
" Which, as in the time of her better health and
mine owne younger judgement," he wrote of it

acidly, ten years after leaving, " I never greatly
admir'd, so now much lesse." He found himself
critical of the scholastic curriculum, which he
considered tedious and out of date, of his instructors, who no doubt enforced it, and of his fellow-
students, whom, not to put too fine a point on it,
he despised. He was disappointed at the inade-
quate supply of intellectuals with which the
University provided him. He did not find there,
as he wrote in his third year to his old schoolmaster, any learned conversation such as his
(Gill's) had been. These ignorant young men
who surrounded him took their flight to theology
knowing nothing, so that Milton was gravely
afraid that the clergy would decline into the
priestly ignorance of times past. As to himself
(he continues), he found in Cambridge scarcely
any companions in study.

That he was not curious to conceal his views
on this delicate topic, or on that of the defects in
the curriculum, we may infer from allusions in
his academic orations to a certain hostility that
he had inspired among his fellows. " How can
I hope for your good will when, in this so great
assembly, I see almost as many hostile faces as I
see heads ? " he demands in a College oration.
It is true that he imputes this to the " rivalry of
those who follow different methods in study " ;
but this is seldom, among young men, a sole and
unadulterated, or even a chief, occasion of un-
popularity. As to his tutors, some hostility there
is scarcely surprising when we read his diatribes
on the education they dispensed ; as, for example,
his attack on the study of scholastic philosophy,
delivered in the Public Schools, when he assured
his hearers that the books they had to study

Bм

served no useful purpose whatever, which must
have been pleasant hearing for his professors
and tutors. What good, continued the dis-
putant, could there be in those altercations of
crabbed old men, that smelt of the monkish dens
where they were written? How much better it
would be were they to study the countries of the
world, the manners of men, the nature of living
things. In a later prolusion, in Defence of
Learning, he complains that the teachers of logic
and rhetoric talked like savages and babies, and
were more like finches than men. Ignorant
gownsmen, monkish itch, the empty rhetoric of
mathematicians, the vile jargon taught in the
jurisprudence schools, all came under his lash.
Spirited orations; but if he made them, or any
part of them, also in his interviews with his tutor,
the fact that from this gentleman he "received
some unkindness" ("whipt him," adds Aubrey,
briefly, but this has been decided to be a lie) is
scarcely odd. A natural rebel and propagandist,
he flung himself into the battle for a more liberal
culture with the ardour and the heat which in
later life he was to bring to his attacks against
bishops, Presbyterians, and those who traduced
his character or condemned divorce for incompatibility. A contentious youth, he thrashed
about him with the flail of his Latin oratory, that
left the heads of his victims bloody but, it seems,
unbowed.

It is tempting, but would be unscrupulous, to
reconstruct the quarrel between the argumenta-
tive undergraduate and his tutor, who perhaps
perceived that his pupil considered him a bar-
barian, a savage, a finch, and almost as contemp-
tible as a monk. Whatever the scene, it ended,

as such differences will, to the pupil's disadvantage ; he was, apparently, in his second year, rusticated. He sustained his brief exile with spirit, indeed with proclaimed pleasure, if we are to judge from his *Elegia Prima*, addressed to his friend Charles Diodati, in which he boasts his good fortune in being in London, for Cambridge is ill suited to Apollo's followers, nor is he inclined to put up with the threats of a harsh master and other intolerable things. He is enjoying his exile, his leisure for reading, and is often at the theatre, on which he dwells in delighted detail. He also sees in the streets bevies of girls who seem to him of exciting beauty. The necessity of " keeping his end up " about his rustication, and probably his angry reaction from Cambridge, embellishes feminine London for him so greatly that he proclaims the wisdom of fleeing from it quickly before Cupid shall wound him.

It seems that he did so, without missing a whole term, was put under another tutor, and pursued his studies. He was writing a certain amount of verse. From the year 1625–6 (his eighteenth) we have surviving six Latin poems (mostly elegiac) and one English, the lovely, though in parts youthfully imitative, *On the Death of a Fair Infant Dying of a Cough*,[1] written of his niece ; a charming blend of Pagan and Christian mythology, with its lavish casting of the infant for the alternative rôles of a star fallen by mistake and replaced by careful Jove, a goddess fugitive from heaven, Mercy, Truth, Astrea, or an angel taking temporary human form. The infant's mother could take her choice among all these, and rest

[1] Mr. J. H. Hanford places this a year earlier. See *Review of English Studies*, July 1933.

assured that if she curbed her sorrow she would
have offspring that would make her name famous
for all time. It seems that she did curb it, for
the brothers Edward and John Phillips arrived
to her.

Milton's other poems of this year were in Latin.
Deaths were frequent in those plague years ;
elegies always in demand. We have four from
Milton, including one on Bishop Andrewes of
Winchester (of whom, when turned anti-episcopal,
he wrote with less esteem). They are formal,
accomplished and competent, and Milton's stock
as an elegist must have stood high. He produced
also some bombastic, tongue-in-the-cheek stuff
about the Gunpowder Plot, for Guy Fawkes' day.
There is little personal expression in any of this
Latin verse, except the rustication poem. They
seem formal exercises. The Latin tongue, so well
adapted for stately compliments or execrations,
fadged well with Milton's natural grand manner. ·
How far in it he expressed his feeling, how far
followed a convention, who shall say ? Are we
to take as authentic the fervour of his first love
poem, written in May, 1628, in which he relates
how, among the *turba dearum* that walked the
roads of the city (for young women walking
abroad were used to seem goddesses in his sus-
ceptible eyes) he had perceived one in particular,
much like Venus in appearance, and Cupid had
forthwith wounded him in a thousand places ;
he burned, he was all a-flame ! He had not
seen her again ; he was, like all lovers, *miser
suaviter*, delightfully miserable.

Whether this was all an exercise after Ovid
and Buchanan, or whether it records an actual
incident, it certainly indicates susceptibility. The

ten lines of lofty contempt for such past vanities,
which he later attached as an epilogue to this
poem, rather point to its genuineness. Socratic
learning, he declares, has cured him of love's
folly ; his breast is now ice (Milton's gift of
seeing himself as he desired seldom failed him).
" He resolved " (to quote his eighteenth-century
biographer, Jonathan Richardson), " Love should
thereafter give him no further trouble. But he
was mistaken. . . ." Indeed he was. For " he
was not," as the biographer justly observes, " in-
sensible of beauty." His next Ovidian poem, the
lovely *In adventum veris*, written the following
April, still shows him a lover, but in general, not
in particular, and is most joyfully full of frolicking
satyrs, pursuing Pans, and imperfectly fleeing
dryads. Between these two poems are some
more academic orations, one the famous *Vacation
Exercise*, part Latin prose, part English verse.
The Latin is a little self-conscious ; the speaker
refers to an improvement in his popularity, and
announces that he has to-day to praise mirth,
though he confesses that he is not very able for
jests. Nor was he. Milton trying to be bois-
terously funny (despite the very pretty satirical
wit recorded of him by contemporaries), was,
throughout his life, a spectacle something inele-
gant. Here, as on later occasions, he stooped to a
vulgarity sanctioned by custom but significant in
him who spoke with such distaste of boorish
bawdry and praised *festam et mundulam urbanitatem*.
This ribaldry may have been part of his protest
against the nickname of " Lady," which Aubrey
says was given him for being " so fair and clear,"
but for which, as Milton suggested, there may
have been other reasons. Was it, he petulantly

enquired, because he could not drink heavily, or because his hands were not hard with ploughing, or because he did not prove his manhood by debauchery? But, he added, ever happy to compare himself with the classical great (with Ovid in rustication, with Pindar " when the assault was intended on the city," with Tiresias in blindness), Demosthenes himself was called by his enemies not enough of a man.

This oration was followed by the English poem beginning " Hail, native language," in which he rejects

> . . . those new-fangled toys and triming slight
> Which takes our late fantasticks with delight,

and throws out suggestions for various fine cosmic themes for English verse, proposing that his mind should

> . . . at Heav'n's dore
> Look in, and see each blissful Deitie.

All through life spying on the gods was one of his favourite dreams ; in the Spring elegy, a year later, he re-dreams it – *Et mihi fana patent interiora Deum*.

At the appropriate time the eloquent and poetic undergraduate took his B.A. degree, subscribing " willingly and *ex animo* " to the three Articles of Religion – the King's supremacy, the lawfulness of the Episcopacy and of the Book of Common Prayer, and the agreeableness to the Word of God of the thirty-nine articles. Whether any or all of the three yet stuck in his throat, we can only surmise. He was, he tells us later, already

turning from the Laudian discipline of the
Church, and resolving against taking orders.

By Christmas, 1629, his poetical development,
swirling in rapid eddies, had led him to the
Nativity Ode. This exciting hymn, too rich, as
some think, in irrelevant ornament, too baroque,
too many-conceited, is a magnificent burst of
emotional vitality and luxuriant imagery. It is
not markedly nor exclusively Christian in tone.
It is decorated not only with the Heav'n-born
Child, and the Shepherds in a rustick row,
helmed Cherubim, sworded Seraphim, and
bright-harnest Angels " all about the Courtly
Stable," but with Nature and the Sun her lusty
paramour, the Halcyon brooding on the sea,
mourning Nymphs, moaning Lars and Lemures,
Apollo, mooned Ashtaroth, Tyrian maids, the
Sun with his chin pillowed upon an Orient wave,
fettered ghosts and yellow-skirted fayes flying
after night-steeds. These creatures are introduced
with loving exuberance ; a " damned crew,"
such as Comus led, forms, in the run of the verse,
the pattern of some magnificent figure dance.
Milton seemed to have thought the poem composed in a mood of ascetic austerity, if we are to
judge from his *Elegia Sexta*, addressed to Charles
Diodati the same December, in which he speaks
of the ode, and of the austere life and spare diet
(herbs and water is his suggestion) necessary for
those who would write of gods and heroes, of
heaven and hell. But there is no austerity about
the rich riot of the *Nativity* ; rather the turbulent
intellectual and emotional ecstasy of the young
man spreading the wings of his genius, and in
love with poetry.

If, as seems possible from his remarks to

Diodati, he underwent at this time some experience akin to religious self-dedication, its
poetic inspiration did not see him through the
following Lent, when he began (but fortunately
left unfinished, finding the subject " above the
years he had when he wrote it ") his very poor
poem on *The Passion*. Here indeed was a spiritless
descent from the splendour of the Christmas Ode,
" But headlong joy is ever on the wing," and the
Passion, a topic which never much interested
Milton, could not re-capture it for him. " Nothing satisfi'd with what was begun," he wrote of it
later. Let us be grateful for so much self-
criticism, but it should have gone further, and
deposited *The Passion* in the fire.

Its badness may have temporarily cooled his
religious-poetical ambitions, for we get no more
in this kind for the present. Instead, he runs
after nightingales and May mornings. Both the
May Song and the Nightingale Sonnet imply
country surroundings and a holiday mood, and
were probably written in 1630, when the University was emptied from spring to autumn by the
Plague. If botanists should protest against

> *The Flowry* May, *who from her green lap throws*
> *The yellow Cowslip, and the pale Primrose*

as retarding this last flower somewhat (May
Day, of course, was our May 12th), one might
remind them in the first place of the exigencies
of rhyme, and in the second, that Milton, though
the country made him poetically joyful, even
went to his head, was never a precise observer of
its floral or faunal detail ; the skipping Pans and
dryads perhaps confused him. *May Morning* and

O Nightingale are lovely with the loveliness traditional and yet spontaneous of a young man's " propitious May." That in some lines of both he echoes his predecessors, and even himself, matters little.

The *Nightingale* shows him again in lover's mood. He followed it with a series of Italian sonnets, telling of his sudden love for a beautiful black-eyed Italian lady. " Diodati (and I tell it thee in surprise), I, who used to scorn love and laugh at his snares, have now fallen. . . . " The laughter Milton imagined ; his attitude towards love had always been one either of excited receptivity, or of defiant fear. Anyhow, he is in love again, or pretending to be so, and it makes an excellent pretext for experimenting in Petrarchean sonnets and practising his Italian. The dignified, idealised passion, and the simple *naïveté* of his account of the excellence of his own disposition, are engagingly Miltonic.

An experiment in a very different mode, of the same year, is the epitaph on Shakespeare, published anonymously two years later, among other complimentary poems, as a prefix to the second Shakespeare folio. It was perhaps their public occasion that gave the lines their peculiar modish intellectual skill : the young man's " wonder and astonishment " are, as it were, marbled in a monument curiously wrought and show that, when Milton wished to emulate " our late fantasticks," he could do it as well as any of them. The conceits are alive and lovely with imaginative passion, and remind us again of how little this poet was ever, except politically, ecclesiastically and controversially, a Puritan. Never so, anyhow, in his attitude towards the arts.

Through his final two years at Cambridge, he
was writing occasional verse – three epitaphs,
two on old Hobson, the University carrier, in a
rare and engaging vein of mixed humour and
affection, and the lovely lines on the death of the
young Marchioness of Winchester. At the end
of 1631, that shock which a twenty-third birthday
administers to most persons of vanity, conscience
or sensibility (more particularly when they reflect
on the occasion by night, and Milton owns these
lines to be " nightward thoughts "), elicited from
him

> *How soon hath Time the suttle theef of youth,*
> *Stoln on his wing my three and twentith yeer !*
> *My hasting dayes flie on with full career,*
> *But my late spring no bud or blossom shew'th,*

a severe judgment on a writer already so fruitful,
though as yet unpublished. He began his twenty-
fourth year in a mood of stern moral and intellectual ambition.

Nothing he ever wrote is more characteristic
than the Latin declamation he delivered in his
College Chapel during this year on the thesis
" Learning brings more blessings to man than
Ignorance." Here he was on his own chosen
ground. He expounds the Platonic doctrine of
the immortal and divine spirit in men, whose
welfare is to be sought in the instructed contemplation of ideas. " Sine arte mens nostra
tota infrugifera est et injucunda." There is, in
fact, no true happiness in life for the unlearned,
and small virtue, though the unlearned may
sometimes be good if they follow the example of
some more erudite being. He paints a distress-
ing picture of a barbarous world without the

arts, as Europe seemed to him to have been but a few centuries ago, in the illiterate Middle Ages, when "nothing was heard in the schools but the foolish dogmas of extremely stupid monks" (a dialogue between Milton and Roger Bacon, or Thomas Aquinas, should have been arranged by Landor). He turns from his scourging of savage ignorance to a rosy picture of the joys of learning – intellectual friendships ; knowledge of astronomy, biology, history, geography, spirits and daemons. The pleasures of fame he says he omits, but, nevertheless, rolls them sonorously out – to be an oracle of nations, to be the guest of kings and republics, to be visited from near and far – the ideal of earthly bliss which haunted him through his life, and for whose sake he wrote so much of what he wished to say in a tongue common to the learned of all nations. He descends from these happy thoughts to deal with our first progenitors wandering beast-like with crouched forms through the wilds, sleeping in dens, religionless, lawless, cultureless, like the beasts around them (a more scientific view of our evolution than it pleased him to take when he came to write *Paradise Lost*). Then with " *Quid autem ignorantia ?* " he opens his broadside on this most despicable of vices and pulverises it. But let us, he eagerly pleads, set ourselves rationally to master some new learning each day, until, like Alexander, we weep that there are no more worlds to conquer.

It was in this mood of Renaissance ambition that he must have left Cambridge, after taking his M.A. degree, in July, 1632.

CHAPTER II

It was probably with relief that Milton shook the dust of his University from his feet, free at last to study in his own way, uninterrupted by tiresome tutors, the levity of ignorant young men, and the irritation of time-wasting declamations in the schools. He had (or so it seemed to him later), after a few early, stormy passages, received favour above any of his equals from the learned Fellows of his College, who signified how much they would like him to stay on. But Cambridge he had never greatly admired, as indeed he had frequently pointed out while he was up there. Now, one imagines him thinking, for real work ; now to read and write poetry uninterrupted ; now, little by little, to win that cycle of universal knowledge which should be a man's true quest, and to attain which God had shaped his capacities.

It has scarcely been enough noted what an original choice of a path in life for an ambitious young graduate and poet Milton made at this time. Not in rejecting a profession : many young poets with indulgent parents and strong wills are able to do this ; but in deliberately isolating himself, avoiding the literary coteries, the University wits, who have in all ages loved to flock about in bevies, encouraging (or discouraging) one another to write, gossiping about books and men

and women, creating and setting up a standard
which they make the literary mode of the hour.
Milton did not want such encouragement or
companionship. He set himself in seclusion to
train his powers for whatever work he might do.
Other literary men might and did praise the
country, summon one another to " leave the
chargeable noise of this great town," say " Fare-
well, ye city wits that are almost at civil war,"
declared themselves weary of " the beauties of
the Cheap, and wares of Lombard Street," and
determined to spend no more of their days to
gain an idiot's praise. But there is no evidence
that Randolph, who thus said, had more than the
country week-end habit ; " Then let's flock
hither," he writes, in other mood, " like birds of
a feather. . . ."

Poor Herrick, who, owing to his cure of souls,
had really to live in the country, would at any
moment have exchanged it for the city. The
young men with literary aspirations who were
Milton's contemporaries – Suckling, Denham,
Carew, Davenant, Waller and the rest – found, as
literary young men have mostly found, before
and since, that London air and conversation, and
not seeing overmuch of their relations, was
favourable to their progress. But John Milton,
with his admirable self-sufficiency, arranged himself at Horton, Bucks, with his elderly parents,
and when he went to London it was to buy books,
hear music, and improve his mathematics, not
to mix with literary society. Others sang of the
pastoral life ; he lived it. (Anyhow for a time ;
it must be admitted that he had tired of its " inconveniences " and " obscurity " in a few years,
and desired chambers in town.)

Milton has left us no part of his life without
news. The controversial tracts of his political
period decorate their bellicosity and adorn their
hate by continual outbursts of splendidly, or
sometimes lamentably, egotistic autobiography.
He not only tells his foes how he has always pursued virtue virtuously, but recounts his intellectual and literary development. He has left his
brief summary of these years at Horton. " On
my father's estate I enjoyed an interval of uninterrupted leisure, which I devoted to the perusal
of Greek and Latin authors ; though I occasion-
ally visited London, to buy books, or to learn
something new in mathematics or music." His
was the leisure of the self-dedicated student. The
young ladies of the Horton neighbourhood, however stirred by the arrival among them of the
handsome and graceful youth, with his " gentle-
manly affability," his " delicate tuneable voice,"
and his brilliant Cambridge reputation, must soon
have perceived that they were not in him to
acquire a playmate. Doubtless they not only
admired but liked him when they met him.
" He was extreme pleasant in his conversation,
and at dinner, supper, etc., but satyricall," says
Aubrey. One hopes that he was not too satyricall
with his parents and country neighbours, who
were no doubt as ignorant as most country neighbours. But he was probably too busy " perusing
the Greek and Latin authors " to see much of
them. Not, however, too busy to take his walks
abroad through the peaceful landskip, delighted
with its charms, a pleased spectator of country
dances and of the hunt careering by, a somewhat
fanciful observer of nature, apt to confuse sweet
briar with honeysuckle. It is notorious that poets

are apt to look, when they walk abroad, rather with the eye of fancy than of precision, on what they see. They take the whole world of poetry, history and geography for their province, and ramble in it at will. Anyhow, Milton, his time spent mostly over his books, did so. His mind, released at last from academic preoccupations, went exuberantly pastoral, partly, doubtless, owing to the change to bucolic surroundings and the excitement of living in, not merely visiting, the country ; partly from the influence of the pastoral poets, Latin and English, and, in chief, of Spenser. Elizabethan bucolics were in the nation's blood. Milton, far more Elizabethan than ` Caroline in literary vassalage, had drunk deep from boyhood, of the Spenserian, as well as the Castalian, fount ; and at the beginning of the Horton years seems to have come still more under this spell.

The most assimilative of poets, he waves his borrowed leaves on every bough ; he plucked them in every garden, English, Greek, Latin, Italian, that he trod. Pastoral was the fashion ; he was steeped in Ovid, entranced by Spenser ; he had been reading Browne, and it amused him, perhaps, to take an idea for his blithe twin poems from the verses which prelude Burton's *Anatomy*. Having noted all this, we come to the poems themselves, and are held enraptured, despite the classical population which foots it resolutely through them, the *turba deorum* and *dearum* which usurp the English fields, the Roman nymphs that dance among the shepherds and milkmaids. To Milton they are all one, all part of the lovely pageant of country life. Among them, his happy young man walks at sunrise in a landskip decorated with green hillocks, elms, whistling ploughmen, singing milkmaids, shepherds counting their sheep beneath hawthorns. Cloud-capped mountains rise, enchantingly Alpine, above the trim meadows of the Home Counties, where hay-making, dancing, eating, drinking and story-telling, merrily proceed. Then the gay young gentleman visits the city, and attends tournaments, plays, masques, frequent and ornate weddings, and, always, concerts.

The graver young gentleman of the *Penseroso* is of a more nocturnal habit : his delights are lunar, stellar, philomelan, sitting up all night to read Plato, Hermes Trismegistus, Greek tragedy and a little modern, the *Squire's Tale* and the *Faërie Queene*, and sleeping in a wood by day. When he visits cities, it is to walk in cloisters, or to attend " Service high " in some richly decorated cathedral, with pealing organ, anthems and quire. An æsthetic, intellectual, sensuously ritualistic young man, who means in old age to turn botanical and astronomical hermit, and end a prophet. Neither he nor his more lively complement seems to do any writing.

The brilliant eldest son, in this pleased mood, must have been a prized addition to his parents' home, though the retired scrivener does seem to have registered some natural paternal protest at his son's reluctance to adopt a profession. He is indulgently answered in the delightful Latin verse epistle, *Ad Patrem*, which very agreeably indicates the relations between father and son. The son explains that poetry is all the thanks he can render, and desires his father not to despise it, since Phoebus has divided his gift of music and poetry between father and son. His father (obviously there had been a little trouble between them) only pretends to hate the muses. He has given him a liberal education, and has not exhorted him to go money-getting. He will sit among laurel wreathes, removed from the lazy, stupid, and profane, and all the *fœdissima turba*. "So, dear father, since I cannot repay your kindness, let it be enough that I have here commemorated it and will always bear it in mind ; and that, if my youthful verses should dare to hope for immortality, your name will be preserved for an example." Whether Mr. Milton compounded for immortality or not, the matter would appear to have been settled, and John remained at Horton undisturbed.

Others besides his father seem to have exhorted him to do some work, for there exist among his manuscripts two drafts of an interesting letter addressed to an unknown friend who had, it seems, admonished him that time was passing on and he dreaming away his years in the arms of studious retirement, like Endymion with the moon. Milton, in answer to this charge, sends him the Petrarchian stanza he had written on turning twenty-three, and explains that he is tardy in order to be more fit. He defends himself against the charge of an idle and curious love of learning, for this would not have held out thus long against the so strong oppositions of every kind, such as ambition, desire for gain, and that " much more potent inclination which about this time of a man's life solicits most – the desire of house and family of his own." The admonishing friend had apparently been urging him to decide on taking Orders, for, perceiving that he may be growing tedious, he neatly concludes, " This, therefore,

C M

alone may be a sufficient reason for me to keep as I am, lest, having thus tired you singly, I should deal worse with a whole congregation, and spoil all the patience of a parish."

In truth, it is certain that by this time Milton had no mind to the ministry ; he wanted (though not saying this) to devote himself to literature and to poetry. Some nine years later, in *The Reason of Church Government*, he throws a backward light that may be in part true, in part lit to meet a later mood, on his anti-ordination resolves – "The Church, to whose service . . . I was destin'd of a child . . . till comming to some maturity of yeers, and perceaving what tyranny had invaded in the Church, that he who would take Orders must subscribe slave, and take an oath withall, which unlesse he took with a conscience that would retch, he must either strait perjure or split his faith. . . ." It had always been necessary, of course, for candidates for the priesthood to take oaths ; what Milton meant, in 1641, by calling himself "Church-outed by the prelates" was that he disliked the particular *kind* of prelatical tyranny which obtained. As often, he may have been reading back. He makes no mention in this letter of any such reason against taking Orders ; it is pretty obvious that he did not want, or feel himself fitted for, the ministerial life, and that he did intensely and passionately desire that of the scholar and poet. He was not "Church-outed by the prelates," but by his own inclinations. And he was right ; he would have made a most strange clergyman. He did also, like most men, distaste the then state of the Church, becoming, under Laud's energetic rule, more ceremonious, closely-governed, and

persecuting, year by year, as the resolute little
Archbishop " moved " (as Fuller wrote) " rather
ascendendo than descendendo on his course,"
dividing the clergy into O. and P. (Orthodox
and Puritanical) for the information of the King.
It was certain that young Milton would not wish
to be stigmatised either O. or P. by the arbitrary
little Bishop from whom preferment flowed,
and whose zeal " gave a sharper edge " to the
ferocious sentences inflicted on ecclesiastical
delinquents. The nagging jurisdiction of the
High Commission Court, and the episcopal censorship of the press, must have seemed to the
unbiddable young man peculiarly idiotic and
offensive, though he was as yet no Puritan, except in the most moderate meaning of that many-
sensed word. Nor had he as yet anything to say
against the Anglican liturgy, nor even anything of
what he was to express five years later in *Lycidas*
about the place-scrambling and ignorant shepherds, the blind mouths that scarce knew how to
hold a sheep-hook.

The friend of this letter was possibly no poetry-
lover, for nothing is said to him of the occupation
which is exalted and justified in *Ad Patrem*, and
which was, in fact, occupying Milton's mind at
the time when it must have been written. There
is no certainty about dates here, and no compul-
sion to follow the order of the drafts in the Trinity
Manuscript, but he had probably, when he
wrote this letter, composed not only the *Allegro*
and *Penseroso*, but the nobly festal *At a Solemn
Musick* ; and was near to putting envious Time,
the subtle thief of his youth, in its place with the
magnificently contemptuous retort *On Time*,

> *And glut thy self with what thy womb devours,*
> *Which is no more then what is false and vain,*
> *And meerly mortal dross ;*
> *So little is our loss,*
> *So little is thy gain,*

ending in the glorious burst of triumph :

> *Then all this Earthy grosnes quit,*
> *Attir'd with Stars, we shall for ever sit,*
> *Triumphing over Death, and Chance, and thee O Time.*

If he could retain such a mood, he was not likely
to let himself be hustled, either by admonishing
friends and relations, or by his own hungry
ambitions, into premature action.

Meanwhile, he was reading voraciously the
great literature of several languages, ancient and
modern. How much of the work of his own contemporaries he read, we do not know. Did he,
from those expeditions to London booksellers,
return with new poetry or plays, with the latest
Ben Jonson, with George Herbert, Quarles, or
Donne, with the *Poetical Blossoms* of young Cowley,
the Westminster schoolboy, or some new mis-
cellany of anonymous verse ? Did he see the
new plays, Ben Jonson's *Magnetick Lady*, and his
last masques, Tom Carew's masque, *Cælum
Britannicum*, Ford's succession of tragedies, or
Shirley's comedies ?

That he read many of the moderns is improb-
able, since he nowhere alludes to them. Ben
Jonson we know he reverenced, though he was
never " sealed of his tribe " ; William Browne and
the Fletchers and other Spenserian-pastoral poets
influenced him ; but the literary crowd that hung

round the court and stage he probably troubled
little about. They went their way, and he his.
Deep in the Greek and Latin, medieval and
Elizabethan writers, he could spare little time,
and had little taste, for the moderns. Like every
one of his generation, he knew Burton's *Anatomy*.
Bacon and Selden he studied for information,
and he must almost certainly have read Mon-
taigne's Essays, and the widely popular Donne.

With one literary mode of the hour, the pastoral-
classical-Arcadian, he certainly kept in touch. It
was probably at Henry Lawes's request that he
wrote *Arcades*, that delicious brief masque that
was to be part of an entertainment acted before
the Countess-Dowager of Derby at Harefield. It
shows Milton in the *Comus* mood, but lighter, and
not dominated by the conquering-chastity theme.
The slight, gay *Arcades* is all sylvan loveliness and
poetry ; *Comus*, a year or so later, not quite all,
for besides being sylvan-classic it is Platonic-
Spenserian. The *Faërie Queene* has entranced its
author's imagination ; victorious chastity has
enspelled him. The chivalric romances of
Christendom had been among his early reading,
" from whence even then I learnt what a noble
vertue chastity sure must be, to the defence of
which so many worthies by such a deare adven-
ture of themselves had sworne. . . . Thus, from
the Laureat fraternity of Poets, riper yeares and
the ceaseless round of study and reading led me to
the shady spaces of philosophy, but chiefly to the
divine volumes of *Plato*, and his equall *Xenophon*.
Where if I should tell ye what I learnt, of chastity
and love, I meane that which is truly so, whose
charming cup is only vertue, which she bears in
her hand to those who are worthy. The rest are

cheated with a thick intoxicating potion, which a certaine Sorceresse, the abuser of loves name, carries about. . . ."

The *Apology for Smectymnuus* is not an amiable document, but for this and a few other passages we can forgive it.

The sources of *Comus*, its connections with other Comus masques and fantasies, with Browne, *The Faithful Shepherdess*, *The Faërie Queene*, the Circe myth, and Platonic doctrines of chastity, have been traced with industry for which such outlines as this book have no place. *Comus* was written to be performed at Ludlow Castle before the Earl of Bridgewater, by his two young sons and daughter, their friends or connections, and the musical composer and director of the masque, Henry Lawes. Pastoral masques were all the fashion ; the Puritan disapproval of them, and of the Queen for having played in one, voiced so recently and so savagely by Prynne in *Histrio-Mastix*, had but stimulated their popularity with court and gentry.

The central theme of *Comus* is the magical power of virginity. How far Milton himself held for a time this mystical theory seems uncertain. He well may have[1] ; on the other hand, it is not fair to load poets with the burden of all they say in song. That Milton had a romantic admiration for celibacy needs no pointing out : it is implicit in much of his work before his marriage ; after this event, the chastity he extols becomes exclusively pre-marital ; even the angels seem to be disallowed celibacy. It is highly likely that at

[1] See E. H. W. Tillyard's *Milton*, Appendix C, for an interesting discussion on this, and its relation to Milton's theory of the audibility of the music of the spheres to the chaste. See also J. H. Hanford's *Youth of Milton*.

the *Comus* period, he had resolved to live un-married, dedicated to study and to poetry. If so, this exaltation of virginity would be character-istic enough. The Lady in *Comus* is, anyhow, a very type of " the sun-clad power of Chastity," and by her boasting of it, succeeds in making Comus as nearly uncomfortable as the gay creature can be.

Comus, despite his serious and obvious faults, is, I think, the most attractive being in Milton's repertory, except possibly the jocund hero of *L'Allegro*. There is a spirit and grace about him, inherited from his two charming parents, that makes one feel that the Lady must have required all her defences to resist him. Beside her and her two budge young brothers, he speaks like an adult man of the world ; his poetry pours forth in entrancing eloquence, while the Lady's is often a little wordy, and her brothers, those prating young princocks, spin theirs out in hum-ourless smugness that tempts one to speculate on the pretty pair of figures of fun, mocked and mimicked by some Mercutio or Beatrice, that Shakespeare might have made of them. But Milton's comparative humourlessness was proof against the egregious pair, and they discourse their way through the Arcadian woods in lines of inimitable priggish solemnity, that must have given immense pleasure, as spoken by the Egerton boys, to the gay and courtly audience. But, if they might smile at the talkative brothers, they must still have been delighted by the ravishing performance. Indeed, slow in move-ment as it is, and full of lectures, moralising, and artificial lumber, it has an exquisiteness that Milton was not to find again.

Till *Samson Agonistes*, nearly forty years later, *Comus* was Milton's one dramatic experiment. It seems always to have been one of his ambitions, among the many that filled his mind and note-books, to write a great drama. Whether he ever believed peculiarly dramatic gifts to be among " the gifts of God's imparting, which I boast not but thankfully acknowledge," or whether he realised his own intense subjectiveness too well for this, he has not left on record.

Comus is the last work of the earlier, happier years of the Horton period. After it, a certain restless unease is discernible in his few letters. " The interval of leisure " took a new colour ; it became what he recalled later as " the wearisome and studious watchings wherein I have spent and tired out almost a whole youth." Ambition, scarce as yet begun to be fulfilled, pressed hungrily on him. Studious retirement, even though he was, as he hoped and believed, thus preparing himself for the work of an immortal poet, was not enough. The troubled affairs of the country were on all tongues. These were the King's eleven happy years (paid for so dearly later) of freedom from his troublesome parliament, when he was gathering money where and how he could, annoying all his subjects by taxation, fines and ship-money, and all but the Laudians by the bullyings of the High Commission Court and Star Chamber. What Milton thought of it all we can only infer from his later attitude towards such things, from his inborn and Greek-nourished love of liberty, from his anti-clerical outburst in *Lycidas*, and from the prevalent tendency of the extracts he copied out between 1635 and 1639 in that one Commonplace Book of his which we have. Direct utterances from him on politics at this time are wanting. Just before the performance of *Comus*, Prynne suffered his savage sentence for *Histrio-Mastix*, and Milton's instinct for liberty must have been outraged, even though Prynne had reviled his beloved drama. Nor can he have approved the Puritan-hunting, the tracking down and bullying of the poor little conventiclers and sectaries who were increasing like rabbits over England, and who abounded in Buckinghamshire. Milton had probably no particular sympathy with these ignorant and oppressed unfortunates, except that their stubborn perversity may have appealed to his own, and his anti-clericalism have burned in him at their persecution. Anyhow, what with religious and what with political tyranny, it was difficult for his active mind not to become increasingly involved in the study of affairs. And we have the evidence of his Commonplace Book that this was so. In this book (one, probably, of several such) he transcribed from his reading notes and references that struck him as interesting, or which were to assist him in some future work. He later used a great number of these extracts in those political and controversial tracts which he describes as " the fruits of my private studies," and one may note the germs of many of the civic and religious ideas which later infected him. There is, for instance, a quotation from Justin Martyr on the permission by the Jews of polygamy, which has been held to indicate that this happy condition had already been conceived by him, and was not called into being later by the hardships of his conjugal career. There are notes on the relations of kings and subjects, taken from the Roman historians,

ecclesiastical and secular, on taxation, and on
clerical affairs (as, for instance, the marriage of
the early clergy, the poverty of early British
bishops, and clerical avarice, as noted by Dante).
Other quotations are from Constantine on human
reason, from Dante on education, suicide and
sloth, from Ariosto and Procopius on alms-giving
and pestilence, from Tertullian on gluttony and
public performances, from Clement on lying
and the modest dressing of women, from Cyprian
on virgins, from Cantacuzenus on gymnastics.
It will be seen that Milton's reading during these
years covered a varied field, and that those books
which he went up to London to purchase can have
been no light matter to carry home. Besides
Italian and Byzantine history, he got through
numerous histories of the Church and several of
the Christian Fathers. All this ecclesiastical
reading is interesting, as showing an early preoccupation with theology and with church as well
as civic government. In the *Apology for Smectymnuus* he gives his 1642 view of the results of his
ecclesiastical studies. They had, he says, con-
vinced him of the iniquities of the Church –
" Some years I had spent in the stories of those
Greek and Roman exploits, wherein I had found
many things both nobly done and worthily
spoken ; when comming in the method of time
to that age wherein the Church had obtain'd a
Christian Emperor, I found it all quite contrary ;
excepting in some very few, nothing but ambition,
corruption, contention, combustion. . . . "
As to the Councils, of which he had been
accused of ignorance, he admits that he had only
" read into them," not wishing to be such a
prodigal of his time as to read the lot. For, he

reasonably argued, seeing how trivial and tedious
were the actions of most bishops singly, " then
certainly united in a Council they would be much
worse," and " to set out the whole extent of their
tattle in a dozen volumes would be a loss of time
irrecoverable " – a point of view with which many
students of the Councils will sympathise.

Anyhow, what with the Fathers, what with
secular and ecclesiastical historians, what with all
the other authors and subjects which occupied
him, and notes from which he doubtless filled other
Commonplace Books (there was perhaps an
exclusively theological note-book, which would
have been valuable as throwing light on that
interesting subject, the development of his religious views before 1641), he seems justified in
referring rather plaintively to the " wearisome
and studious watchings " of these years. Except
these notes from books, the only writing we have of
Milton's between *Comus* and 1637 is a short Latin
letter to his old schoolmaster, Gill, in December
1634, making an engagement with him at the
bookseller's for Monday and sending him a trans-
lation of the hundred and fourteenth Psalm into
Greek heroic verse. Then, in September 1637,
after, apparently, some epistolary remissness on his
friend's side, he writes to Diodati, now a doctor,
rather querulously upbraiding him for his silence
and for his forgetfulness to pay him a promised
visit. His tone, peremptory and rather complaining,
and showing real feeling, suggests a state of over-
wrought nerves that might well be produced by
over-work, solitariness, deferred ambition, and
country and family life too greatly prolonged.
There is also that note of egotism and of a somewhat swollen vanity that belonged to his temper,

and which could only probably have been cured by some years of knocking about the world among men of his own generation and education, who would argue with and contradict him. If he never attained, in his maturity, to the stature he might have reached, if he was quarrelsome, domineering in controversy, curious rather to make scores off his opponents and to exalt himself and his party than to examine a question judicially and arrive at truth, if the sweetness known to his friends never played its due part in his public utterances, the fault lay partly with the " times most bad," partly with his natural temper, and partly, perhaps, with those retired, self-cultivating years in his father's home.

The solitude, hard study and obscurity had now begun to drag and irk. He would soon be turning twenty-nine, and still so little done, and all the world untasted while he laboured over his books at Horton. His mother, too, his *mater probatissima*, had died in April of this year. Thenceforth he was alone with his father. The scrivener was now over seventy ; one may imagine that he missed his wife of thirty-seven years' standing and was a tired, sad man, no companion for his erudite and ambitious son, who loved him with grateful affection, but had possibly not much to talk about with him. Intercourse with one's mother was different ; she smiled at one's jests, admired one's gifts, believed in one's greatness, and saw to one's comfort, and, in turn, one cherished and loved her. But where was the use of being " extreme pleasant at dinner, supper, etc.," alone with an elderly and bereaved scrivener, who could not enter with any spirit into the philosophic and literary discussions for which the intellectual of one's own age are apt?

After his mother's death Milton seems to have definitely decided, what he had for some time suspected, that his retirement at Horton was reaching its term. He says as much in his next letter to Diodati. This letter is a little cumbersome in its attempt to repartee Diodati's cheerful Latin wish that he might be well six hundred times; more than a little when he proceeds to discourse on true friendship maintaining itself despite lack of letters, and to commend his friend's superior character. But his tone changes, mounting from priggishness to fine Platonic emotion, and with it to humility, as he goes on, " It is impossible not to love such as you. What else God has ordained for me, I know not, but this is certain, he has given me a strong love of the beautiful." Wherefore, when he found one who, scorning the vulgar, followed the best, to that man he must needs attach himself. Even were he, with all his efforts, destined never to be such an one himself, he must still look up to those who had attained that glory. (And this is one of the few really humble things about himself that Milton ever wrote in his life; it is both a high tribute to his friend's character and some evidence of his own temporary self-despondency.) " But," he goes on, reviving somewhat, but still gracefully humble, " you ask what I am thinking of? Let me boast in your private ear. Of immortality, God help me! I am growing my wings and preparing for flight; but as yet my Pegasus only rises on very frail wings; let me be humbly wise." Leaving this subject, he tells Diodati that he is thinking of leaving the country and moving to London, into one of the Inns of Court, where he will live more conveniently, have companions at hand when he stays at home, and more stimulation when he goes out – " here, as you know, I live obscurely and confined."

After all, he was to have next spring a better change from his cramped life, and far finer stimulation, than rooms in the Inns of Court would have afforded, for he was to go travelling on the continent.

But before that, in November, he wrote *Lycidas*.

Between *Comus* and *Lycidas* lie over three years of poetical silence.[1] The poet, having created the lyric magic of *Arcades*, and the grave beauty, interwoven with lovely and naïve absurdity, of *Comus*, was apparently content to spend three years after them (and doubtless more, had not the external stimulus of the elegiac volume for Edward King spurred up his tender-winged Pegasus into one brief flight) in silent study, in preparing himself to write that which should bring him immortality. It may be taken as a symptom of slowness in gestation, of close application to other studies, or of ambition ridden on the curb. Milton was not to be hurried, even by immortality. He could write poetry and knew it ; he might at once have published a slim volume of English and Latin poems which would have given him some reputation. But he preferred to wait. " *Volare meditor*," he wrote to Diodati, using a word which leaves it doubtful whether he was practising flight, or only thinking about it. He wrote nothing, anyhow, in those years, that he chose to publish in his 1645 volume.

[1] Unless we follow Professor Grierson, who gives some good reasons for placing *Ad Patrem* between them.

Ready elegist as he had always been, we have nothing on the death of his mother in April 1637, nor on any of the many deaths from plague. He who had be-dirged his infant niece, old Hobson, Lady Winchester and Bishops, seems to have renounced dirges. Among the tragic ironies of Milton's life is this, that, during the years when he was capable of *L'Allegro, Il Penseroso, Comus,* and *Lycidas,* years never to return, he wrote no more such poems. When youth's sweet-scented manuscript closed for him, it was only a few exquisite, sparsely written sheets.

On the last sheet was inscribed *Lycidas,* " of which the diction is harsh, the rhymes uncertain, and the numbers unpleasing," wrote Dr. Johnson, with his customary firmness. Neither does it contain passion, " for passion runs not after remote allusions and obscure opinions. . . . Its form is that of the pastoral, easy, vulgar, and therefore disgusting." He proceeds to dispose of the poet's absurd statement that he and King had shared bucolic pursuits, for " we know that they never drove afield and that they had no flocks. . . . He who thus grieves will excite no sympathy. . . . The poem has yet a grosser fault. With these trifling fictions are mingled the most awful and sacred truths, such as ought never to be polluted with such irreverend combinations."

Foolish criticism by the great is perhaps sometimes worth quoting, since it lends to the thing criticised that freshness which is staled by unmitigated praise. Such a view of *Lycidas* from an erudite being gives a sharper edge to our own appreciation. When Johnson says *Lycidas* lacks passion, its lines throb for us again with their quivering protest against youth cut down in its prime, against the blind Fury (as he angrily miscalls Atropos the Fate) and her abhorred shears, which rob laborious, dedicated youth of its longed-for guerdon of fame. It scarcely needs to say that it is his own youth, his own guerdon, his own possible death, that so moves him, rather than poor King's.

> Fame *is the spur that the clear spirit doth raise*
> (*That last infirmity of Noble mind*)
> *To scorn delights, and live laborious dayes ;*
> *But the fair Guerdon when we hope to find,*
> *And think to burst out into sudden blaze,*
> *Comes the blind* Fury *with th' abhorred shears,*
> *And slits the thin spun life.*

Through the lines cry the conflict and effort of those laborious, ascetic, striving Horton years, that have sometimes been spoken of as peaceful. They must have been just about as peaceful as a Marathon race. Indeed, did Milton ever feel peaceful for more than an hour or two on end, even when strolling in fine weather in the Buckinghamshire fields ? For he could accept nothing calmly, and least of all the limitations of others.

Crashing and snarling like an angry lion into the lament for Lycidas comes St. Peter, shaking his mitred locks and emitting his hymn of hate against the clergymen of England who sit at home at ease though Lycidas, their better, must perish, who only care for their bellies, who scarce themselves know how to hold a sheep-hook, or have learned aught else the least. Thus St. Peter, foreshadowing many later diatribes of Milton's

on the theme, and bitterly echoing the old undergraduate contempt – " they fly off unfledged to
theology, while all but rude and uneducated."
Milton's fears for the future of these young men
had, it seems, now been realised.

The dread (and, one fears, rather prejudiced)
voice of the Pilot of the Galilean Lake ceasing,
the lovely final section of the elegy begins, like
quiet music after storm. We are among the
radiant flowers of Sicilian and English pastorals ;
the lost shepherd meanwhile is washed by the
tides, visiting the bottom of the monstrous world,
and so, after all, to heaven, to be entertained by
sweet societies of saints, to become at once a soul
in glory and the Genius of the perilous flood – a
combination of trifling fiction with the most
awful and sacred truths which Dr. Johnson found
unspeakably improper.

So, in high and lovely tranquillity, triumphing
over Death and Chance and thee O Time, the
dirge ends. The sun sets ; the poem is done ;
to-morrow to fresh woods. That line of emotion
and thought is, for the present, ended ; that
account with envious Time for the moment settled.
Now for fresh work – or perhaps what the uncouth
swain refers to is his projected change to rooms in
the Inns of Court.

Not, probably, the continental trip, for, writing
to Diodati only a little before this, he has not yet
made this plan. Whenever it was made, our poet,
complete with passport, man-servant, funds from
his obliging father, elegant letters of introduction
to eminent foreigners, as much knowledge of the
Italian language as was needful, and more than
enough of the history of Italy, started on his
travels in April 1638, going first to Paris, where

Dм

the English ambassador entertained him and
introduced him to Grotius, then busily trying to
bring the Church of England into a Pan-Pro-
testant Union. Thus passed on from one intro-
ducer to another, the personable young poet
appears to have made a triumphant social progress
through France and Italy, reaching Florence
("which I have always particularly esteemed for
the elegance of its dialect, its genius, and its
taste") in July, and remaining there for about
two months, entertained by the politest people
in the world, attending the literary gatherings of
"many truly noble and learned men." Thus
surrounded by beauty, antiquity and welcoming
literati, he must have felt, after the narrow years
at Horton, that he was at last in a congenial
world. His hosts and he talked of literature, of
learning, of the censorship of the press, of politics,
and Milton talked of his religion, and, we fear,
of theirs, to which they, with Italian politeness,
listened, and, with Italian cynicism, very likely
agreed. They and their English guest, nothing
loth, read one another their poems at the meetings
of the academies, "for," wrote Milton later,
recalling these happy travels of his in *The Reason
of Church Government* (it is well not to ask how the
subject of his own past triumphs came into such
a theme), "the manner is that everyone must give
some proof of his wit and reading there." The
"trifles" which Milton read "were received
with written Encomiums, which the Italian is
not forward to bestow on men of this side the
Alps" (here he wrongs the courteous Italians).
So delighted was he with their reception of his
Latin verses that he was strongly tempted to bid
for continental fame by writing in future mainly

in Latin. Fortunately, either at the time, as he seems to imply, or on his return to England, out of sound of those charming Italian encomiums, wiser counsels prevailed, and he returned to the decision expressed long since in " Hail, native language," and to his aspiration after the office of national poet. But, despite his decision to forgo international fame to this extent, " not caring to be once named abroad, though perhaps I could attain to that," he must often have felt a longing, among his relatively unappreciative, often hostile, countrymen, for those magnificent Southern compliments, some fine samples of which he prefixed to the Latin poems of his 1645 volume, in the vain belief that the printing of such enthusiasm would improve his position with his readers, or merely because the temptation not to waste such good matter was irresistible.

The compliments of Italians flow like honey ; his friend Dati's address to him has the uncompromising fervour of an epitaph – his intellect, his perfect knowledge of tongues, his beauty, virtue, eloquence, astronomy, philosophy, history, everything – no wonder Milton could not bear not to print it, together with the equally gratifying Italian ode by Signor Francini, which assures him that the profoundest secrets which nature hides in heaven and earth are clearly known to him, that he has attained the limits of moral virtue, and that his sweet song has exalted him to heaven. Even allowing for the politeness of a Florentine gentleman, Milton in Italy had obviously made a good impression. He was taken to visit old Galileo in his villa outside Florence – " I found and visited the famous Galileo, grown old, a prisoner to the Inquisition for thinking in

astronomy otherwise than the Franciscans and
Dominicans thought." He was, in fact, taken and
introduced everywhere. After Florence, he had
two months in Rome, where, besides " viewing
the antiquities," he received the most friendly
attentions from learned and ingenious men. In
a grateful letter afterwards to the Vatican librarian, Milton thanks him for his courtesy, and
particularly for giving him access to " the most
excellent Cardinal Barberini," of whom he speaks
in gratefully enthusiastic terms which he may
have recalled with embarrassment two years later.
Indeed the courtly friendliness shown him in
Italy by so many of the faith he never ceased to
revile might have hampered a lesser man in his
theological diatribes, at least while still in their
country. But Milton seldom allowed such con-
siderations to cramp his style ; he admits that,
at Naples, he embarrassed the distinguished old
Marquis Manso, who " was exceedingly friendly.
. . . On parting, he excused himself that, though
he had desired to offer me more attentions, he
could not do so in that city, because I had not
been more reserved about religion." And, " when
I was about to return to Rome, some merchants
warned me that the English Jesuits had prepared
snares for me because I had spoken too freely on
religion. . . . Nevertheless, I returned . . . and
for another two months I again very freely
defended the reformed religion in the very city of
the Pope." He was not going to allow himself to
be " bejesuited," whatever cordiality and esteem
might exist between him and cardinals, whatever
magnificent musical entertainments they might
offer him, entertainments of which he has recorded
his appreciation in his three short poems of

enthusiasm to the famous singer Leonora Baroni.

Having thus enjoyed and made himself agree-able at Rome (for his personal charm, if any further evidence were required than the recorded testimony of those who knew him personally, the social success of his Italian tour seems to supply it) he proceeded to Naples, falling in on the road with an eremite, who performed for him a friendly office which, one hopes, took him out of the pack of " Embryos and Idiots, Eremits and Friars " relegated in *Paradise Lost* to the Paradise of Fools, for he introduced our tourist to the great Manso, Marquis of Villa, patron, at seventy-eight, of letters, art, culture, and youth. Milton found him a kindly cicerone and friend, and addressed to him a fine hexameter poem of thanks, in which he politely suggests that even the dark and arctic England has had, and still has, its poets. He wishes himself such a friend as Mansus, patron of poets, who would, when he died, see to his worthy burial and have have him carved in marble, with a wreath. It is a handsome tribute, full not only of poetry and politeness, but of British patriotism, for he speaks proudly of the Druids, of the three British nymphs hymned at Delos, and of his pro-ject of writing an epic of King Arthur. In return, Manso presented the young poet with two en-graved cups, and wrote him an epigram – If thy religion were even as thy mind, form, grace, face, and disposition, not only English but angelic thou wouldst be. This, too, naturally enough, found a place among the prefixes to the 1645 volume of poems.

Probably to his lasting disadvantage, Milton never got south of Naples, where he was checked by news of troubles at home. England and

Scotland, he heard, were all of an uproar, Scotland having overturned Episcopacy and the King making ready for the Bishops' War ; so, " I thought it disgraceful, while my fellow citizens fought for liberty at home, to be travelling for pleasure abroad." But there is also a hint in the *Epitaphium Damonis*, written after his return, that he had had about enough of travel by now ; he speaks of Thyrsis brought home from Tuscany by his *mens expleta*, his satisfied mind, as well as by *pecorisque relicti cura*, the care of his abandoned flock.

It was a lamentable decision, this victory in Milton of the patriot over the tourist, this forgoing of Sicily and Greece, to return to what he calls his Arctic native land, there to join in those passionate quarrels that heated and inflamed the minds, if not the bodies, of its denizens, and which summoned him from afar as the trumpet's call the war-horse.

The war-horse, however, would appear to have been in no hurry, for he spent some six months more in Italy, and dallied a while in Geneva with the learned professor of Protestant theology, Giovanni Diodati, the uncle of his friend Charles (who had died last August, four months after Milton had left England). There also he found Alexander More, Franco-Scottish professor of Greek, More the calumniator, the liar, the adulterer, who seduced the maid-servant of his host, who succeeded in behaving in a debauched manner even in the predestinating city by the lake, whose alleged infamy provoked, and resounds through, the *Defensio Secunda*, because Milton believed that he had published a calumny on himself. Whether, while practising in Geneva the dual function of

Professor of Greek and Calvinist Pastor, Mr. More
was, or was not, actually observed by the stern
eyes of the English visitor to be behaving so ill as
the latter came later to believe, it seems that
Geneva had, anyhow, its temptations, for Milton,
when alluding to his stay there, calls God to
witness that in none of those foreign cities where
vice is so freely and so shamelessly practised, had
he practised any ; and this we may readily believe.

CHAPTER III

THE POET TURNED PAMPHLETEER

MILTON returned to his country, after an absence of a year and three months, when the second Bishop's War was starting with Scotland, and English political troubles were well under way. But our poet did not at first do anything about these. Possibly, after the excitements of abroad, England dropped him down to earth with a heavier bump than he had anticipated. He was saddened by Diodati's death, now that he had time to realise that he had lost his dear and only intimate friend, to whom he would have related with so much pleasure the saga of his travels, telling him of the Florentine young men; of Roman society; of the Jesuits whom he had defied, speaking most freely of the superior merits of his own communion; of the literary tributes with which he had been be-garlanded; of his plans for writing in future great poetry in English.

All he could do was to write an elegy to his friend, telling him dead what he could no longer tell him alive. The *Epitaphium Damonis*, that beautiful and characteristic dirge, " written," to quote Dr. Johnson again, " with the common but childish imitation of pastoral life," is Milton's last poem, in either English or Latin, for some years. It is, perhaps, the final word of his youth.

As not in *Lycidas*, here he is mourning the loss of a

friend, and, under the guise of the two shepherds, is able to describe their friendship as the daily companionship it had never, since schooldays, been – " Whom shall I trust with my soul ? Who will bring me again thy caressing ways, thy laughter and the Attic salt of thy wit and fancy ? " Probably no one ever did, and one may guess that the miss of his friend's jesting humour was to be more intellectual and moral loss to Milton, who could ill spare it, than he knew.

He was not going to be baulked by death of telling Diodati about Italy, or about his poetical plans. After an outburst of bitterness that he had been unnecessarily abroad while he might have been seeing the last of his friend, he tells him about his travels, and makes then a sudden and characteristic turn aside from Thyrsis to Milton and his plans, his intention to write an epic of British history and legend, and to write poetry in future in English. But the British epic with which he was great was never born ; he confesses that he had made a false start at it some days since, and perhaps he never made a good one ; possibly Arthur was driven from his mind by politics, by his growing disapproval of monarchs and those who fought for monarchs, or by his schoolmastering. For whatever cause, the Arthurian tale remained a mere suggestion in his note-book. The brave promise of a life dedicated to English poetry rides through the *Epitaphium* with the pathos of a gallant ship that is never to come to port.

There is a less obvious hint in this poem, that the thought of marriage haunted the writer's mind. The maidens tell Thyrsis that youth by right seeks love, *bis ille miser qui serus amavit* –

twice wretched is he who has loved late. To this Thyrsis makes no direct reply. But he closes his lament with a picture of Damon in heaven recompensed for his earthly virginity by immortal nuptials, " where the lyre mingles wildly with the beatific dancing, and feasts and orgies rage under the Thyrsus of Sion." This is a more exciting heavenly portion than was assigned to Lycidas, who was to hear the unexpressive nuptial song, entertained by solemn troops of saints. Damon is rewarded with a positive orgy of heavenly weddings. " At least," Milton seems to cry, with an almost conventual rapture, almost as Crashaw might cry it, mingled with a Bacchic fervour that Crashaw did not know, " he shall have all the nuptial ecstasy with which heaven can compensate those who have been undefiled on earth." " *Fame* is no plant that grows on mortal soil," he had bravely, if unconvincingly, written two years since ; and now he sought, equally unconvincingly, to make the same valiant claim for love.

It is apparent to us, possibly it was apparent to him, that Milton was about ready to think of getting married.

But at present he was full of plans for work. " I hired for myself and my books a large house in the city, where I happily resumed my interrupted studies," is his account. His nephew Edward mentions a preliminary lodging in St. Paul's Churchyard, " where he first undertook the education and instruction of his sister's two sons." Dr. Johnson spitefully looks " with some degree of merriment on the man who hastens home because his countrymen are contending for their liberty, and when he reaches the scene of action, vapours away his patriotism in a private

boarding-school." The eighteenth century regarded schoolmasters as a bad joke, though
Johnson adds that for Milton to earn money in
this way was " an act which no wise man will
consider as in itself disgraceful." In any case,
Milton does not offer this handle to his foes in his
own account. He says that he settled himself to
study, and trusted in God and the people to bring
the public troubles to a right issue.

In point of fact, he was both studying and
teaching. He had his own ideas of a liberal
education. " Nor," says Edward Phillips, after
a formidable list of some of the books in which the
pupils were instructed between the ages of ten and
fifteen or sixteen, " did the time thus studiously
employed . . . hinder the attaining to the chief
oriental languages, viz., the Hebrew, Chaldee,
and Syriac, so far as to go through the Pentateuch
in Hebrew, to make a good entrance into the
Targum, or Chaldee Paraphrase, and to understand several chapters of St. Matthew in the
Syriac Testament." Also some Italian and
French ; and for Sundays the Greek Testament.
The optimism that characterised Milton's youth
and middle age seems, in this curriculum for small
boys, to have had full scope ; and one may feel
moved to echo Dr. Johnson's comment, " Nobody
can be taught faster than he can learn." Or, as
Edward Phillips humbly expressed it, " Had they
received his documents with the same acuteness
of wit and apprehension . . . as the instructor
was indued with, what prodigies of wit and learning might they have proved ! " They might
even have fulfilled the promise their master had
made at seventeen to his bereaved sister, that her
future offspring " till the world's last-end shall

make thy name to live." No such felicitous result
came of the Phillipses' education, though they
grew up adequate translators of several languages
and skilled in music. Of the other scholars' subsequent careers, we know little; possibly they
were frightened off learning by their boyhood's
ordeal, and became low of brow for life, as John
Phillips became decidedly low of mind.

The teacher was also " perpetually busied in
his own laborious undertakings of the book and
pen." He moved very soon into the " pretty
garden-house in Aldersgate Street," where he
could have his considerable library, and some
more scholars, and plunged with ardour into his
studies. His nephew allows him one sociable
relaxation – " Once in three weeks or a month he
would drop into the society of some young sparks
of his acquaintance, whereof were Mr. Alphry
and Mr. Miller, two young gentlemen of Gray's
Inn, the Beaus of those times, but nothing near so
bad as those nowadays. With these gentlemen
he would now and then keep a gawdy day."

Meanwhile, when not thus engaged, he resumed
the entries in the Horton Commonplace Book.
Largely they bore on English history, in which his
interest was freshly roused. There are many
extracts from the chroniclers, bearing mainly on
a few groups of topics – monarchy, republics,
laws, taxation, tyranny, freedom of the press,
marriage, and so on. There are ecclesiastical
citations from Savonarola and ethical ones from
Lactantius. But, on the whole, his preoccupation
at this time was with history.

The Commonplace Book entries should be
collated with the seven pages of jotted notes in the
Trinity manuscript, wherein he copied the drafts

of his poems.   In these pages, probably in the
years 1639–40, he set down, as they occurred to
him, possible subjects for epics and plays.   It is
obvious that his Arthuriad, the idea of which had
so attractively and strongly beset him in Italy,
was not getting on even yet.   If it was still a pro-
ject, it had to take its chance among about a
hundred others.   Milton was, as a poet, very
slow off the mark.   His desire to wait till he had
" completed to my mind the full circle of my
private studies," before committing himself to
poetic expression on a large scale was not only
patient self-restraint ; it had an element, almost,
of intellectual disease.   Some ninety-nine Biblical
or historical subjects are noted down by him
about this time.   The list is headed by the Fall,
for which Milton gives two alternative synopses.
In the main, he keeps pretty near in scheme to
the epic of twenty years later, though the lists of
dramatis personæ include, besides Adam, Eve,
Lucifer, etc., personified qualities, as in the Mor-
ality Plays.   It is no disparagement of *Paradise
Lost* to wish that this drama had been written.
Lucifer would have been as imposing a villain as
ever stepped the boards, Adam and Eve must have
been as delightful beings as they are in the epic
(but what would they have worn in the pre-fig leaf
stage ?   This consideration may have been among
those which changed *Paradise Lost* into a poem),
and the serpent would have been the most engagingly sinister of great tree worms.   But it was
not to be.   Nothing, drama or epic, was due for
writing yet, and, had it been so, the Fall would
have had to compete with Abraham, Sodom (to
be entitled *Cupid's Funeral Pile*), the Golden Calf,
the Quails, David (Revolted and Adulterous),

Solomon Gynœcocratumenos, Herod massacring, Christus Patiens, and twenty more themes from scripture, besides all those from history, such as the Massacre by Hengist of the Britons in their cups on Salisbury Plain ; Edwin for lust deprived of his kingdom by a faction of monks and the impostor Dunstan ; Edward, son of Edgar, murdered by his stepmother ; Brightrid poisoned by his wife Ethelburga, who dies miserably in beggary, after adultery in a nunnery ; Hardiknut dying in his cups, an example to riot ; Duff and Donwald, a strange story of witchcraft and murder discovered and revenged ; Macbeth ; and many more, among which, however, Arthur and his Round Table are not.

That to create some great poem or drama out of English history, as well as out of Hebrew, was a project dear to Milton at this time, we have his own word in *The Reason of Church Government*. He relates here, in one of his interesting bursts of confidence, his uncertainties in selection of a literary form – " Time servs not now, and perhaps I might seem too profuse to give any certain account of what the mind at home, in the spacious circuits of her musing, hath liberty to propose to her self " – whether to try an epic, and if so, what about ; or a drama ; " Or . . . to imitat those magnifick Odes and Hymns wherein Pindar and Callimachus are in most things worthy. . . ." Or, he seems to suggest, lyric poetry. " For these abilities, wheresoever they be found, are the inspired gift of God rarely bestow'd . . . and are of power, beside the office of a Pulpit, to inbreed and cherish in a great people the seeds of vertue and public Civility. . . . And what a benefit this would be to our youth and gentry, may be soon guest by what we know of the corruption and bane which they suck in dayly from the writings and interludes of libidinous and ignorant Poetasters. . . ." And so forth. It says much for the poetic genius of this teacher of his country that, under the weight of all his sermonising, he succeeded in writing any more poetry at all.

It was some time before he did so. These were stirring times, and our poet was now to embark in prose on the " troubled sea of noises and hoarse disputes," and to endeavour to save his country by pamphlets. The Long Parliament met in November 1640. The abolition of bishops was debated ; Bishop Hall wrote his *Humble Remonstrance,* and Smectymnuus replied to it. Smectymnuus, as everyone knew, was five Puritan divines, of whom Milton's old teacher, Thomas Young, was the largest contributor. A very rain of pamphlets began ; it was like the rain of frogs in Egypt. Among them came in the Summer of '41 an anonymous tract called *Of Reformation touching Church Discipline in England and the Causes that hitherto have hindered it.* It was Milton's first pamphlet ; the gun that opened his long tractarian warfare. Before it goes off, it seems the moment to enquire into his motives for thus abandoning his literary projects and so lengthily and closely embattling in the cause of Root and Branch.

He himself gives them at some length, as they appeared to him to be, in *The Reason of Church Government,* and in the *Defensio Secunda* (1654). In the later passage he describes how " when liberty of speech began to be allowed, all mouths were opened against the bishops. . . . At this I was thoroughly awakened, when I discerned . . . that from these beginnings would proceed the delivery

of all human life from slavery. . . ." He decided
that now, if ever, was the time not to be found
wanting to his country and church. So though
his thoughts were elsewhere, he transferred them
to this urgent cause.

The English passage is fuller. In it he laments
the burden of knowing more than other men and
of having to pass it on, more particularly when it
will give offence. "But when God commands to
take the trumpet and blow a dolorous or a jarring
blast, it lies not in man's will what he shall say."
If he should be silent, God would for ever reproach
him for accepting leisure and ability for study
" out of the sweat of other men," and using it only
to adorn vain subjects ; " but when the cause of
God and his church was to be pleaded, God
listen'd if he could hear thy voice . . . but thou
wert domb as a beast ; from hence forward be
that which thine own brutish silence hath made
thee." If he were seeking vain-glory, this, he
says, would not be the manner, the matter, or the
time of his writing. Even were he ready to write,
" it were a folly to commit anything elaborately
compos'd to the carelesse and interrupted listen-
ing of these tumultuous times." Neither would he
choose to write prose, wherein " knowing my self
inferior to my self, led by the genial power of
nature to another task, I have the use, as I may
account it, but of my left hand." He then recounts the history of his literary development and
of his various plans for a great work, which, he
pledges himself, he will yet accomplish when the
time is ripe, and when the land has " enfran-
chised her self from this impertinent yoke of prelaty, under whose inquisitorious and tyrannical
duncery no free and splendid wit can flourish."

Although, he ingenuously protests, it contents him nothing to disclose his plans thus, he does so to show " with what small willingnesse I endure to interrupt the pursuit of no lesse hopes than these, and leave a calme and pleasing solitarines, fed with chearful and confident thoughts, to embark in a troubl'd sea of noises and hoars disputes." But still, he must obey God's Secretary, conscience ; and more particularly since he had been destined when young for a clergyman.

These reasons for turning pamphleteer were, no doubt, genuine. But the reluctance that he believed himself to feel is more doubtful. He was a born fighter ; here were matters in which he was deeply interested, and he threw himself into battle with ardent, if unconscious zest (one of the more entertaining passages in his self-revelations is that in which he declares himself to be over inquisitive in self-examination). He no doubt enjoyed helping his friends the Puritans and the good cause, annoying the bishops, fighting in this stirring battle, and using for missiles the fruits of his ecclesiastical and historical researches.

Of Reformation reads more calmly than some of the later tracts, as if its writer were not yet so exacerbated by battle as he rapidly became. Not that it is gentle – far from it. " Manybenefice-gaping mouths " and " canary-sucking and swan-eating palates " are among the less unpleasing features of which he complains in the clergy. And it would be hard to surpass the violence of his closing objurgation, in which he begs for the bishops a shameful end in this life, and promises them that they shall after it be thrown down eternally into the darkest and

Eᴍ

deepest gulf of hell, there to remain for ever,
" the trample and spurne of all the other
Damned."

In the main, *Of Reformation* is an epitome of
church history and abuses as Milton saw them.
The church has left its primitive purity. Yet it
never had any, since apostolic times. Milton gets
a little confused, in his desire to have it all ways;
much the modern bishops, he ironically says,
would like the holy fasting, prayers, and poverty
of the primitive episcopacy to which they appeal ;
besides, the primitive episcopacy was already
corrupt. Bishops are a mistake ; but anyhow, the
bishops of to-day are not bishops. The church
was already " in a universal tetter of impurity "
before the time of Constantine, who completed
the job of corruption. And so forth. He tells the
tale of the arrested English Reformation, which
had never come to maturity owing to the evil and
worldly dispositions of prelates and sovereigns.
Cranmer, Ridley and Latimer may have been
martyrs, but what of that ? They were unfaithful
shepherds, and but half-hearted Protestant reformers, and why should martyrdom excuse
corrupt doctrine and discipline and a liturgy
extracted from the mass-book ? And after them
the English church had gone from bad to worse,
though there seems, from Milton's sketch of its
past, to have been scarcely room for this.

The point that chiefly strikes one in this pamphlet is the acrimonious dislike of the whole
episcopal bench that has sprung fully armed to
meet the occasion. Milton's researches into
church history had left him able to say, " Ever
since their comming to the See of Canterbury,
for near twelve hundred yeares, to speake of them

in generall, they have been in England to our Soules a sad and dolefull succession of illiterate and blind guides ; to our purses and goods a wastfull band of robbers . . . to our state a continuall Hydra of mischiefe and molestation." If someone had reminded him of archbishops who had been learned, who had furthered education, or championed the people against king or nobles, he would doubtless have had an answer ready, for he was never at a loss. Episcopacy was to him a many-headed dragon at which he must tilt. " It worsens and sluggs the most learned and seeming religious of our Ministers, who no sooner advanc't to it, but like a seething pot set to cool, reeke out the greatest part of that zeale and those Gifts which were formerly in them, setting in a skinny congealment of ease and sloth at the top." With how many bishops, if any, Milton was personally acquainted, we do not know. But he knew all about them, and about those " free-born Englishmen " who had " been constrained to forsake their dearest home . . . whom nothing but the wide ocean, and the savage deserts of America could hide and shelter from the fury of the Bishops." Touchingly he believed that, directly episcopacy should be abolished, and presbyterianism established, England would become " the city of God," and the good life would automatically break forth through her length and breadth. It is apparent that he had never visited Scotland, nor known many Scots, beyond the good Dr. Young.

One may doubt if he was closely acquainted, either, with many of the sectarians whom he defended ; a conversation between Milton and, .say, a Familist or an Adamite, would have been well worth hearing. He was, indeed, a strange prophet of the unlettered sects. But it was as a prophet that he saw himself ; a singing prophet – " Then, amidst the Hymns and Hallelujahs of Saints, some one may perhaps bee heard . . . in new and lofty Measure to sing and celebrate thy divine Mercies. . . ." A glorious dawn is to break over England, and is not to lack its lark. " Some one may perhaps be heard. . . ." It was an intoxicating picture, the new, liberated, de-bishoped England and her appointed Laureate. Patriotism, religion, idealism combined with egoism to paint it in the richest hues. Milton's gift of identifying himself with the noble and the good was swelling in him, blown up by contro-versial zest and by this new windy pump, the pamphlet. It was becoming self-intoxication ; and to bear this in mind is to understand many things about this strange embattling – the frequent out-breaks of insolent ill manners, the gratuitous passages of autobiography, even the splendour of much of the prose. English prose was, so far as we have evidence, a new toy to Milton (since he seemed to conduct his correspondence mainly in Latin), and he plays with it often awkwardly, flinging up huge sentences, like baroque palaces, to the sky, abandoning them unfinished, starting another, adorning them with gallant jewelled phrases, beating even the seventeenth century at its own game. This first pamphlet is rich in dec-oration ; and, in spite of containing a great deal of nonsense, and some hard (though probably un-conscious) lying, it falls into little of that coarse brutality that all too easily beset its writer, and was to make some of his later pamphlets so dis-pleasing.

Having got his hand in, Milton could turn out pamphlets like a baker making loaves. His second is a dull piece of anti-episcopal argument. His third was evoked by Bishop Hall, author of the *Humble Remonstrance*, who was carrying on a duel with the Smectymnuan gentlemen, into which Milton broke with his *Animadversions*. Here, attacking a particular member of the hated tribe, he quite loses his temper and manners and is both silly and rude, alternating such passages of grave beauty as " Who is there that cannot trace thee now in thy beamy walk through the midst of thy sanctuary, amid those golden candlesticks," with crude slanging-match repartee that lacks even cleverness, and is sometimes reduced to a school-boy " Ha, ha, ha ! " and sometimes to a pot-house " Wipe your fat corpulencies out of our light." Milton trying to jest is a sight to make angels weep. That a man who can write a poet's prose, who can fling out such phrases as " they seek the dark, the bushie, the tangled Forest, they would imbosk : they feel themselves strook in the transparent streams of divine Truth, they would plunge, and tumble, and thinke to ly hid . . ." and " the perpetuall stumble of conjecture and disturbance in this our darke voyage, without the card and compass of Discipline," and " Whatsoever time, or the heedless hand of blind chance, hath drawn down of old to this present, in her huge drag-net, whether Fish or Sea-weed, Shells or Shrubbs, unpickt, unchosen, these are the Fathers," can turn the next moment to stupid, pointless, opini-astic scurrility, must be accepted as one of the tragical oddities of his extraordinary mind.

Early next year he launched *The Reason of Church Government urged against Prelaty*, a dignified,

if something ill-tempered, and certainly over-
lengthy, plea for presbyteries. He attacks the
Prayer Book, again, as " an extract of the Masse
book translated," and falls foul of the late Bishop
Andrewes, whom he had elegised at Cambridge
when his view of bishops had been different,
calling him *semideamque animam*, and dreaming of
him in heaven trumpeted to by angels. To atone
for having seen a bishop in such a position, Milton
now sets him firmly in his place.

But there is a passage more interesting to us, if
not to Milton's readers at the time, than this, or
than his elaborate description of the merits of the
system of church government he would prefer, or
than such bursts of alliteration as " he should
need no other pretorian band nor pensionry than
these, if they could once with their perfidious
preachments aw the people. For although the
prelats in time of popery. . . ." More worth having
than this is the long outbreak into autobiography
at the beginning of the second book, of which
much has been quoted already, as it applied. It
is one of Milton's most characteristic articula-
tions, in its mixture of innocent boasting, ingenuous baring of his soul before a probably
indifferent public (as he had done long ago, a
boy declaiming in the Cambridge schools) and
acknowledgment of the responsibilities of his gifts,
" remembering also that God even to a strict-
nesse requires the improvement of these." Then,
with some faint misgiving, " And though I shall
be foolish in saying more to this purpose, yet . . ."
yet, in fact, he will tell the interesting story of his
early education, his early promise, his success
among the Italian Academies, the duties of the
poet as teacher of his country, his intention to

write his great poem, " a work not to be rays'd
from the heat of youth, or the vapours of wine,
like that which flows at wast from the pen of
some vulgar Amorist."

These open-hearted confidences are continued
in his next pamphlet, bearing the handy title,
*An Apology Against a Pamphlet call'd A Modest
Confutation of the Animadversions upon the Remonstrant against Smectymnuus.*   These pamphlet titles
develop something like the house that Jack built ;
the reply of Bishop Hall and his son to the *Animadversions* was called *A Modest Confutation of a Slanderous and Scurrilous Libell intituled Animadversions
upon the Remonstrant's Defence against Smectymnuus*,
and very rude it was, with accusations that the
writer of the *Animadversions* had spent his youth in
wantonness, been " vomited out " from Cambridge
into a suburb sink of London, where he spent his
afternoons in the playhouses and brothels, and was
now trying to marry a rich widow.

If Milton had required (but he scarcely did) a
pretext for expounding his life and character at
length, he had it in these aspersions.   So he breaks
out again, and this time in excusable dudgeon,
into self-defence, and flings to his foes a wealth of
material for a biography they had no notion of
writing.   Not, he explains at some length, that he
cares for himself, but it is his duty to his cause
and to his friends the Smectymnuans, to clean
his name.   He therefore cleans it with a will,
scrubbing and scouring through several pages.
He tells how, far from being vomited out by the
University, he had won the most gratifying
esteem there.   He gives an account of his mornings, spent in reading good authors and exercise ;
of his afternoons he only mentions that they were

not spent in playhouses or bordellos. Indeed, he implies, rather disingenuously, that the only plays he has seen were the college plays acted at Cambridge.

The bordello charge spurred him on, after some further apology, to the story of his fealty to chastity – " he that would not be frustrate of his hope to write well hereafter in laudable things, ought him selfe to be a true Poem, that is, a composition and patterne of the best and honourablest things. . . . These reasonings, together with a certaine nicenesse of nature, an honest haughtinesse, and self-esteem either of what I was, or what I might be . . . kept me still above those low descents of minde, beneath which he must deject and plunge himself, that can agree to salable and unlawfull prostitution." Of true love, " and how the first and chiefest office of love begins and ends in the soule," he hopes to speak more later, " in a still time, when there shall be no chiding ; not in these noises, the adversary as ye know barking at the door." Finally, he had learnt as a Christian that unchastity must be more dishonourable in a man, the perfecter sex, the image and glory of God, than in a woman, who is merely the glory of man ; and that in heaven there were celestial songs only apprehensible to those who were not defiled with women.

So he closes the case for the defence of his morals, and descending with depressing abruptness from the heights, proceeds to some unseemly and ill-tempered banter about the Bishop's feet (whether Milton or his foes were the ruder in controversy seems to be one of those fine debatable points which it were only painful to dispute).

Having remarked that he would, like other
prudent and elegant men, choose rather to marry
a poor virgin than a rich widow, he rises to
eloquence again in his attack on the liturgy and
the inconveniences and dangers that follow the
compelling of set forms of prayer. " This
Liturgy all over in conception leane and dry, of
affections empty and unmoving, of passion . . .
destitute and barren : besides errors, tautologies,
impertinences." He recalls with pain " where
we found it, whence we had it." Though " it
hath indeed bin pretended to be more ancient
then the Masse," it is really a parting gift from
our divorced wife, Rome, who said at parting,
" Keep these letters, these tokens, and these few
ornaments. . . . Thus did those tender hearted
reformers dotingly suffer themselves to be over-
come with harlots language."

Having thus disposed of the Prayer Book, he
applies himself with even more zest to the avarice
of the clergy, and so ends.

This was the last really triumphant blast he
was to blow. For nothing was to fall out as he
had, with such surprising, such touchingly inexperienced hope, trusted. Presbytery was to turn
out by no means what he had thought it, but to
prove nearly as human, as faulty, as irritatingly
tyrannous, as prelaty. Liberty was not to descend
from heaven to build the city of God in England ;
and he himself was to be caught and trapped, like
a unicorn, by his love for a virgin, and to suffer
wounds in that tragical business that were to leave
him maimed and embittered for life.

THE MUNICIPAL COLLEGE
DEPARTMENT
OF
ARTS
PORTSMOUTH

CHAPTER IV

MARRIAGE AND DIVORCE PAMPHLETS

THE odd and disastrous affair of Milton's first marriage has had of late a little fresh light thrown on it, for it has been pretty well established that it took place a year earlier than we have always been told, and that Edward Phillips's " about Whitsuntide," when his uncle took a journey into the country and returned a married man, was 1642, not 1643. The first Divorce Tract was written and published the following year, after his wife had left him. There are still problems about this marriage, but nothing necessarily bewildering. Milton, having now a house of his own, and being thirty-three years old, no longer saw reason to refrain from that state for which his inexperienced youth had been so unwise a preparation. *Bis ille miser qui serus amavit*; the nymphs had thus addressed Thyrsis in the *Epitaphium Damonis*, nearly three years ago. If he meant to get married, he should be setting about it now. Moreover, he had (one may assume) fallen in love once more with a girl's pretty face and form. The girl was Mary Powell, the eldest daughter – she was seventeen – of Mr. Richard Powell, an Oxfordshire gentleman long known to the Milton family and, apparently, owing them a considerable sum of money. Of Mary we can make only a doubtful picture, guessed at from the brief narrations of the contemporary biographers, and from her husband's embittered comments in the divorce pamphlets on the disappointing mate to whom a man might have the mischance to be tied. From Edward Phillips's and Aubrey's detached, not unsympathetic comments on the young woman's attitude towards her new life and husband, we can at least imagine the situation. Of pleasing appearance she probably was, since Milton liked women to be this, and we know of nothing else to account for his attraction to her. "Dull, mute, spiritless, sullen, unfit for any cheerful conversation," she may or may not have been ; or she may have been so in Aldersgate Street and not in Oxfordshire.

Such as she was, Milton, after a month's absence, brought her home, with a posse of her relatives, and for some days there was nuptial merry-making, which probably bored the bridegroom, but softened for the young bride her advent into so unaccustomed and, as it proved, so distasteful a life. For distasteful the poor girl found it. She had no mind, says Edward Phillips, to " a philosophical life, after having been used to a great house, and much company and joviality." And Aubrey, " She found it very solitary ; no company came to her, often-times heard his nephews beaten, and cry. This life was irksome to her."

In any case, she returned to her family in about a month, promising to be back by Michaelmas, and when Michaelmas came she was not back, and no notice was taken of her husband's messages of summons, except to insult his messenger. Edward Phillips attributes this to the political differences between Milton and the Cavalier

Powells, the war being now begun ; and Aubrey,
more concisely, " Two opinions do not well on
the same bolster." Anyhow, " it so incensed our
Author, that he thought it would be dishonourable ever to receive her again after such a repulse ;
so that he forthwith prepared to fortify himself
with arguments for such a resolution, and accord-
ingly wrote two treatises, by which he undertook
to maintain, That it was against reason . . . for
any married couple disagreeable in humour and
temper . . . to be forced to live yoked together
all their days." " He who had entered into that
state," says another contemporary, " for the end
designed by God and nature . . . could ill bear
the disappointment he met with by her obstinate
absenting : and therefore thought upon a divorce
that he might be free to marry another ; concern-
ing which he also was in treaty. The lawfulness
and expedience of this . . . had upon full consideration and reading good authors been formerly his opinion : and the necessity of justifying
himself now concurring with the opportunity
. . . of instructing others in a point of so great
concern . . . he first writ *The Doctrine and Discipline
of Divorce*, then *Colasterion*, and after *Tetrachordon*."

But all to no avail : the Westminster Assembly
would listen to none of it. Our author remained
for three years " married and yet not married,"
and his " design of marrying one of Dr. Davis's
daughters, a very handsome and witty gentle-
woman," if ever entertained, was never fulfilled.

The first Divorce Tract came out in August
1643, about a year after Mary Powell had fled.
No one reading it but must be moved by its cry
of disappointed pain, its continued harking back
to the frustration of the chief end of marriage,

which was " the apt and cheerfull conversation
of man with woman, to comfort and refresh him
against the evill of solitary life " (him, not *them*,
one must note : Milton's point of view throughout
is the husband's. To a suggestion of any other
he ejaculates " Palpably uxorious ! ") Though
" through their different tempers, thoughts, and
constitutions," they can not live in any union or
contentment, yet they shall " be made, spight of
antipathy, to fadge together, and combine . . .
to their unspeakable wearisomnes and despaire of
all sociable delight."

This is the burden of the whole long tract : and
an age-old grievance and misery has never been
so well set forth. The idealist, who has spent his
youth in celibacy, not squandering his affections
on trivial engagements, comes in due time " to
put off an unkindly solitarines by uniting another
body, but not without a fit soule, to his, in the
cheerfull society of wedlock," looking for " a ready
and reviving associate . . . whereof who misses
by chancing on a mute and spiritles mate, remains
more alone than before, and in a burning lesse
to be contain'd than that which is fleshly, and
more to be consider'd." For " the desire of joyn-
ing to it selfe . . . a fit conversing soule (which
desire is properly called love), *is* stronger than
death . . . many waters cannot quench it, neither
can the floods drown it." Hoping for this love,
a man may have " spent his youth unblamably,"
and neglected such experimenting as may have
brought to the less unblamable a shrewder knowledge of whom not to marry, and now he finds
himself " bound fast to an uncomplying discord
of nature, or, as it oft happens, to an image of
earth and fleam, with whom he lookt to be the

copartner of a sweet and gladsome society, and
sees withal that his bondage is now inevitable ;
though he be the strongest Christian, he will be
ready to despair in virtue, and mutin against
divine providence : and this is doubtless the
reason of those lapses and that melancholy despair
which we see in many wedded persons." "For
what kind of matrimony can that remain to be
. . . when their thoughts and spirits flie asunder
as farre as heaven from hell ? " How can " that
intimate communion of body be held with one
that must be hated with a most operative hatred,
must be forsak'n and yet continually dwelt
with ? " It would be the last betrayal of man
by God, had He intended this. " Did he open
so to us this hazardous and accidentall doore of
marriage to shut upon us like the gate of death
without retracing or returning ? " " Such a disturbance . . . ends, if there be not a miracle of
vertue on either side, not onely in bitterness and
wrath, the canker of devotion, but in a desperate
and vitious carelessness, when he sees himself,
without fault of his, train'd by a deceitful bout
into a snare of misery."

What is he then to do ? " Piece up his lost
contentment by visiting the stews, or stepping to
his neighbours bed, which is the common shift in
this misfortune ? " Or suffer " his usefull life to
wast away and be lost ? " No : he shall " doe
more manly " to end his misery by divorce, " for
to retain still and not be able to love is to heap
up more injury . . . he who therefore seeks to part
is one who highly honours the married life, and
would not stain it."

The interesting part of the pamphlet is not the
ingenious juggling with scriptural texts and

ancient laws, which reminds us that, when Milton
decided against the Law (among other professions)
the courts lost a great special pleader, but the
human cry of pain, and the situation which can
but be guessed at through it. For whatever reason,
Milton had come to see his absconded wife as (to
put it with considerable meiosis) temperamentally
unsuited to him. He had made a bad mistake, and
so had she. He was apparently not able in the
important art of perceiving what a young woman
is like behind her pretty face. Both, perhaps, had
been lured to their doom by a handsome appearance. " The sobrest and best-govern'd men," he
explains, " are least practiz'd in these affairs ; and
who knowes not that the bashfull mutenes of a
virgin may oft-times hide all the unlivelines and
natural sloth which is really unfit for conversation." She may have " a mind to all other (than
bodily) due conversation inaccessible, and to all
the more estimable purposes of matrimony use-
lesse and almost liveles."

A dull and spiritless dunce, he would imply.
Further, a dunce who had not welcomed intercourse with her alarmingly " highbrow " husband,
in the lonely house in Aldersgate Street, but who
had gone home to her merry duncicall family and
the cheerful environment of the neighbouring
military, and had refused to return. But, one
must remember, he had desired her return. When
did he cease to desire it ? How much part did
his humiliation and anger at her refusal play in
the subsequent building up of the " image of earth
and fleam " who is the villainness of the Divorce
Tracts ? How soon did their brief union fester
in his memory as a humiliation, a mere soulless
sensuality, " as if a living soul were bound to a

dead body " ? Had it actually seemed so at the
time ?

Mary's side of the story and account of the
honeymoon is unfortunately lacking. Milton is
his own eloquent counsel ; she has none. He,
in passionate language of often haunting beauty,
has engaged our sympathies for all time with
ideals of marriage many of them so modern that,
even three hundred years after, they are still
unrealised. It is perhaps not fair. There seems,
in this tragic piece, no villain, only two victims.
And Milton's views on the divinely appointed
inferiority of women seem oddly incongruous with
the ideals of marriage to which his wife was
expected to conform. But, no matter how we
judge of the affair, so great is the magic of her
husband's words that Mary Powell has gone down
to history as the mute and spiritless mate, the dull
girl who wrecked a poet's life.

Her limitations were probably accentuated for
him by the companionship of more intelligent
and conversable gentlewomen – the Lady Mar-
garet Hobson, who " had a particular humour
for him and took much delight in his company,"
which must have been consoling ; a younger,
anonymous and rather priggish young virgin, who
" laboured up the Hill of Heavenly Truth " ;
and the handsome and witty Miss Davis. All
these ladies no doubt helped to show up Mary.
But not all their united ingenuity, wit, and labours
with Heavenly Truth seem to have done much
to counteract the opinion of women that he was
to retain through life. He had always known
that women were not much : man was the image
of God, women only the glory of men. His brief
association with Mary had shown him that they

were scarcely even this. " Who can be ignorant that woman was created for man and not man for woman ? " The Spirit of God, through Solomon, had written of bad wives and what a plague they were ; but where had God ever mentioned bad husbands ? He obviously " had more pitty towards man thus wedlockt, than towards the woman." The Spirit also related of Vashti, whose unbiddableness caused the Medes and Persians to " set up a wholsom Law, *that every man should beare rule in his own house.* And the divine relater shews not the least signe of disliking what was done ; how should he ? " How indeed ? The husband might give his wife a bill of divorcement if she should find no favour in his eyes and if he should find some uncleanness in her. And uncleanness naturally included such defects as cause " a perpetual nullity of love and contentment . . . and dead vacation of all acceptable conversing."

Let the husband, then, go to the magistrate, and, on his mere request, let poor Mary " by all the united force of the Decalogue . . . be disbanded."

The whole pamphlet is an extraordinary medley of high ideals, common sense, tortuous reasoning, tragic pleading, priggish oblivion of the wife's point of view, splendid phraseology, modernist appeals to freedom from the letter of the law, medieval appeals to Scripture, and distortion of it for his purpose. Whatever we may make of his relations with Mary Powell, he was certainly now desperate to be rid of her, determined to be so openly and legally, and bent also, in his inimitable manner, on advancing public liberty together with his private ends. He really did believe in

Fm

divorce for incompatibility, and hate and despise
the laws which counted adultery the only crime
against marriage.

The tract had a bad press. Even James Howell,
lying in the Fleet for debt, wrote of it with severity.
The clergy, naturally, were all shocked. So Milton published in February a second edition, pre-
facing it with a long address to Parliament and
the Assembly, in expectant admiration of " the
piety, the learning, and the prudence, which is
hous'd in this place." " Doubt not, worthy
Senators," he exhorts them, " to reach out your
steddy hands to the misinformed and wearied life
of men. . . ." The Senators proved unworthy. It
may have been about now that Milton began to
perceive that new presbyter was but old priest
writ large. It certainly must have dawned on
him that these good men had neither the desire
nor the power to " imitate the old and elegant
humanity of Greece," which he was for ever hold-
ing up before their uncomprehending and dis-
approving eyes. They proved themselves no
more human, elegant, just or free in their attitude towards divorce than were the " crabbed
textuists."

But he persevered. In July he published the
Judgment of Martin Bucer, and next March *Tetrachordon* and *Colasterion*. *Tetrachordon* is mainly
concerned with ingeniously manipulated evi-
dences from Scripture ; though we owe to it some
further vivid comments on the married state, as
that to live with " a minde perpetually avers and
disagreeable, betraies us to a wors condition than
the most deserted lonlines." " They . . . live as
they were dead, or as they were deadly enemies
in a cage together." " That grisly Porter, who

having drawn men and wisest men by suttle allurement within the train of an unhappy matrimony, claps the dungeon gates upon them, as irrecoverable as the grave." " Cleav to a wife, but let her bee a wife . . . not a nothing, not an adversary, not a desertrice ; can any law . . . be so unreasonable as to make men cleav to calamity, to ruin, to perdition ? "

Colasterion deals firmly with an assailant, and has for motto – *Answer a Fool according to his folly, lest hee bee wise in his own conceit.* It proceeds to do so, and adds to folly a violent incivility, far greater than any its author had been offered. His opponent is an illiterate, knowing neither Greek nor Hebrew ; he is a Pork who has read no philosophy ; his doctrine of the chief end of marriage comes out of some stye ; he is a paltry solicitor, a servingman, an idiot, jesting and frisking in the luxury of his non-sense with poor fetches to cog laughter from us, a boar in a vineyard, a snout, an odious fool, an unswilled hogshead, a presumptuous lozel, a brazen ass. " Thus much," concludes Milton, " to this Nuisance." His enquiry, " What language can be low and degenerate enough " to use to such a being, he adequately answers here ; and ends by telling his readers that being attacked gives him a chance to exhibit his " talent of sport, which I had thought to hide in a napkin." Even those most enamoured of Milton's talents must wish that he had risked divine disapproval by keeping this one perpetually in its napkin, and that this master of high ideals and of prose that often rises and falls on the ear like a surging sea had not been given opportunity for such elephantine gambolling and " barbarous noise."

This last, as made by others, he deplores in the pathetic sonnet written soon after the failure of the divorce pamphlets :

> *I did but prompt the age to quit their cloggs*
> *By the known rules of antient libertie,*
> *When strait a barbarous noise environs me*
> *Of Owles and Cuckoes, Asses, Apes and Doggs. . .*
> *But this is got by casting Pearl to Hoggs. . . .*

It being evident that the hogs and the other animals were going, for the present, to have the best of the dispute, hopes for divorce must have been, by 1645, pretty low. If our author really did in this year hope to marry another, he must have meant to take a high-handed line and annul his own marriage, since the law would not do it for him. However, the lady was (somewhat naturally) averse to this notion, which would have placed her in the anomalous position of wife not in the sight of man, nor even of heaven, but of Milton only.

Then, about July 1645, Mary Powell came back. According to Phillips, this was due to rumours of the contemplated new marriage, and to the declining state of the King's cause and of the Powell fortunes. Anyhow, Mary reappeared, and " he was surprised to see one whom he thought to have never seen more, making submission and begging pardon on her knees before him. He might probably at first make some show of aversion and rejection ; but partly his own generous nature, more inclinable to reconciliation than to perseverance in Anger and Revenge ; and partly the strong intercessions of friends on both sides, soon brought him to an Act of Oblivion, and a firm league of peace for the future."

Such is Phillips's brief account. At the true story we can only guess. What passed in Milton's mind, on seeing again, after three years of absence, anger, bitter memories, and ardently sought divorce, her to whom he had referred at such considerable length as one to all the more estimable purposes of matrimony useless and almost lifeless? Did he still think so of her? And if so, how was he willing to enter once more into that " worse condition than the most deserted loneliness "? Did he hope that Mary might be by now improved, be more biddable and agreeable? Or did he merely make the best of a poor business? After all, here he was, apparently indissolubly married, at least in the eyes of other young gentlewomen and their fathers, and here was this girl, in the same bonds, pleading for his forgiveness, protesting (so says Wood) that it had all been her mother's fault. He may have settled down to a life lived on a level which youth had never anticipated, in a mixture of apathy, pity, desire, and cautious hope.

What the seven years the two spent together were like to either, we do not know; only that they had four children. To remember Milton's bitter and so recent words about conjugal union when minds are as far as heaven from hell, his contempt for it as only fit for the beasts, is to be faced with a riddle. How much had the anger of a hurt and humiliated man to do with those high words? Or did he decline from them and submit to life on the dusty plain where it is commonly lived, ceasing to expect marriage to be a vacation of love, contentment, and solacing conversation, accepting it, not as a dungeon, a desert, or a paradise, but as the common exasperating highway of

man, with satisfactions to be found by the way ?
A dull wife, dull children (three girls, and all, it
would seem, rather stupid), a dull and tyrannical
church and state . . . it appeared that life was,
after all, like this.

The interesting question remains, what would
Milton have made of a clever and cultivated wife ?
How would he have fadged with a Dorothy
Osborne, a Lucy Hutchinson, an Anne Finch ?
The anonymous " pork " who had attacked the
Doctrine and Discipline had written – " We believe
you to count no woman to due conversation ac-
cessible . . . except she can speak Hebrew, Greek,
Latin and French, and . . . be able to hold discourse with you. But other gentlemen of good
quality are content with fewer and meaner en-
dowments, as you know well enough." Milton
did not answer this charge. We shall never know
how he would have got on with a wife of these
gifts, or how she might have affected his views of
her sex. Would Eve, had her creator's connubial
circumstances been thus different, have been
another type of woman, perhaps even have been
permitted to sit with Adam and the archangel at
table and join in their cosmic conversation, instead
of merely supplying the fruit and nuts and then
wandering away to do some gardening, knowing
that Adam would tell her afterwards all she needed
to know, and doubtless more, of the table talk ?

This must remain speculation. Milton had
educated women among his friends ; but in the
matter of female education he seems to have been
behind his day. For the treatise in which he has
set forth his educational ideals is entirely concerned with boys. Comenius, the great educational theorist, whose books were making so much

stir when Milton wrote, had followed Plato in
making his system for both sexes alike. Milton, in
whom the anti-feminist prevailed over the Platon-
ist, had not (he admits to Hartlib) read Comenius,
and himself gives no views on the education of
girls. He seems not to have troubled to have his
daughters taught much. It is, of course, possible
that he tried and failed, that they were all
dunces. From what we hear of their grown-up
lives, this seems probable, though not certain.
Alternatively, it is possible, that their father never
gave them a chance, assuming that it would be
nonsense to educate them like rational beings.
Anyhow he was very busy, and left them largely to
servants. But one would prefer to believe that he
tried to impart some instruction to them. After
all, their cousin Edward Phillips's story of their
reading Greek and Hebrew aloud to their father
would, if true, premise some intelligence and
learning, however little they understood of what
they read.

But Milton's relations with his children must be
left, like those with his wife, among the many
unsolved family questions of history. After the
fall of Oxford the Powell family came to stay, and
were, as Milton wrote to a friend in Italy, continually at hand to stun him with noise and waste
him with vexation, while those endeared to him
by community of tastes were almost all withheld
either by death or distance. By that time he had
an infant adding to the noise ; and altogether,
neither domestic nor public life can have appeared very liberal, elegant, or free.

CHAPTER V

EDUCATION, AREOPAGITICA AND HISTORY

BESIDES divorce pamphlets, Milton had written during the year before his wife's return his two most agreeable tracts – *Of Education* and *Areopagitica*. The Education tract was evoked by the request of his friend, Hartlib. He admits it to be but a summary – " these few observations which have flower'd off." They set forth his programme for the liberal education of boys from twelve to twenty-one.

Not all the airy grace with which he describes the hill-side of a virtuous and noble education, " so smooth, so green, so full of goodly prospect and melodious sounds on every side, that the Harp of Orpheus was not more charming," can disguise the fact that his Academies were to be the most laborious cramming-schools that ever afflicted schoolboys. Milton says that the young gentlemen would enjoy it, so much sweeter would be their fare than " that asinine feast of sowthistles and brambles which is commonly set before them." They would master their Latin and Greek grammar in no time, and then some easy Greek books could be read to them, interspersed with such lectures as will enflame them with the love of learning and virtue. " Being perfect in the knowledge of personal duty," they then proceed to scramble up the educational hill-side at a rather breathless rate, mastering books in Latin and Greek on every branch of knowledge, the curriculum stiffening as the young gentlemen get older. " And ere this time," Milton casually throws in, " the Hebrew tongue at a set hour might have been gained . . . whereto it would be no impossibility to add the *Chaldey*, and the *Syrian* Dialect." As a relief, they shall have wrestling, fencing, and so on, and mock wars to teach them the arts of battle, and music to recreate and refine them.

" Thus, Mr. *Hartlib*, you have a general view in writing, as you desire us." We do not know whether Mr. Hartlib replied, " But must they read all their literature, science, geography and mathematicks in Latin and Greek ? " Nor, " Are you not a little over-estimating the powers of assimilation of the average youth ? "

The education tract has been instanced as showing that Milton still, in this period, was hopeful for human nature. The same might be said of *Areopagitica*, written to protest against press censorship. The Presbyterian souls of the Assembly had taken alarm at the flood of schismatical pamphlets that multiplied with the sectaries ; they had not overthrown prelacy to set up liberty, and they perceived that they must act quickly. Hence the new Printing Ordinance, of which Milton took no notice, calmly publishing his divorce pamphlets without leave. He then saw that it was time to do something about freedom of the press, " so that the judgement of what should be published and what suppressed should not be in the hands of a few men, and those mostly unlearned and of common capacity. . . ."

This splendid plea and protest is too familiar

to call for much comment here. It contains some of Milton's finest felicities of rhetoric and phrase, quite his best good sense, the most eloquent eulogies of free choice ever uttered in English (among others, the famous passage beginning " He that can apprehend and consider vice with all her baits and seeming pleasures, and yet abstain, and yet distinguish, and yet prefer . . ."), his best epigrams (such as " a fool will be a fool with the best book, yea or without book "), examples of his most touching and misplaced hopefulness, and of his new disillusionment – " It is not the unfrocking of a Priest, the unmitring of a Bishop . . . that will make us a happy Nation."

Areopagitica burns with the passion for liberty (now kindled to white heat by the censoring of the divorce tracts) that was to disgust him finally with the Presbyterian government.

He still thought, though not long to think, that the English nation was noble and worthy to be free. He had not yet seen through his countrymen ; but he was definitely beginning to see through the Assembly and Parliament. " Episcopal arts begin to bud again " ; he could say no worse. His specious flattery, " your faithful guidance and undaunted Wisdome, Lords and Commons," does not disguise his view of them.

Areopagitica was published with no licence asked for or received. The Stationers' Company called the attention of Parliament to this omission ; but the matter was wisely not pursued – an example of the immunity from justice which was to stand our author in good stead throughout his life.

After the two divorce tracts of March 1645, a lull descended on the pamphleteer. The first Civil War was more or less settled at Naseby in

June. Literature began a little to revive, largely
under the ægis of the cultivated publisher Mosely,
who helped more than any other to keep the lamp
of the muses alight through these disagreeable
years. Among the books of verse that he published
in the autumn of 1645 was *Poems of Mr. John
Milton, both English and Latin, compos'd at several
times*. They were, in fact, all Milton's poems,
from his youth up, which he wished to preserve.
The Virgilian quotation on the title-page makes
it clear that he was anxious at this point in his
career thus to chaplet his brow with the poet's
garland, to stand before the world as poet, not as
pamphleteer. The little volume was adorned
with the compliments of foreigners, and with the
much less complimentary portrait by Marshall,
which annoyed Milton so much that he made the
engraver add to it in Greek a disavowal of its
likeness. The publisher contributed a dignified
and pathetic preface, saying that nothing sells
nowadays but pamphlets.

We do not know what, if anything, the poet's
Puritan friends (and enemies) thought of all this
half-pagan verse, these masques, these songs set to
airs by the Royalist musician Lawes, this clear
indication that the divorce pamphleteer, the rebel
against press censorship, the anti-Presbyterian,
was also a half-profane poet. We know that Dr.
Rouse, librarian of the Bodleian, valued the book
enough to ask for another copy, to replace one
lost. Milton accompanied the second copy with
a charming heroic ode, perhaps the most agreeably modest thing he ever wrote, alluding to his
infertile genius and the zealous but by no means
excessive talent of his youth. Pathetically he
looks back to the youthful poet, as yet *insons*

populi, his feet scarce touching the ground as
he wrote. He is here purely the humanist man
of letters, deploring the expulsion of the Muses
by war. In much the same mood of art-above-
the-battle he wrote, early in 1646, the charming
sonnet *To my friend Henry Lawes*.

But the still reverberating Presbyterian attacks
on the divorce pamphlets brought the poet down
into the arena shortly after this, to write the
famous *On the New Forcers of Conscience under the
Long Parliament* – a typical instance of his combined personal and public spirit in attack. It was
a release of all his never closely pent up irritation
at the tyrannical bigots who would " force our
Consciences that Christ set free " ; it was a
declaration of open war against the presbyters.

After this, Milton, perhaps bored for the moment with controversy, or perhaps merely not
goaded by any personal vexation to engage in it,
and certainly with increasing disillusionment
about and annoyance with practically all his
countrymen, who were beginning to seem scarcely
worth writing pamphlets at, subsided for the time
being into private life. His new house in Barbi-
can was uncomfortable and noisy, that is to say,
it was full at all hours of schoolboys, old Mr.
Milton (who gave, however, no trouble, but spent
his time at rest and devotion), and numbers
of the Powell family, of whom no such convenient
tastes are recorded. Mr. Powell was become a
ruined Cavalier, and settled himself, with wife
and progeny, on his son-in-law, while he compounded for his Delinquency until his death early
in 1647. Christopher Milton, engaged also in this
pursuit, lodged near by. Babies arrived to the
Miltons, adding to the uproar.

Old Mr. Milton deceased soon after the impoverished Mr. Powell, and improved his son's estate by so doing. The school was renounced and " our Author chang'd his great house for one more accommodated to his circumstances, where, in the midst of all the noise and confusion of Arms, he led a quiet and private life, wholly delighted with the Muses." Our author, in fact, moved, in the winter of 1647, to High Holborn. Here he began to write, not indeed his great epic, which still hung fire, as great epics will, but a *History of Britain*. The early British had, as a topic, stood for some years in the south of his favour ; he had a taste for Arthur and for Druids. He begins pretty far back, with the conquest and reign of Albion, son of Neptune, It is a lively, well-told, but almost dateless history, characteristically contemptuous of the story of Boadicea (" as if in Britain women were men and men women ") and of the " absurd and preposterous custom " by which British women had several husbands, as compared with the " liberty not unnatural for one man to have many wives," characteristically inclined to topical analogies and strictures, denunciatory of the national clergy, and disgusted at having, after the withdrawal of the Romans, to " steer by another sort of Authors," barbarous, unreliable, struck with superstition as with a planet – " in one word, Monks."

He makes opportunity to tell the modern civil and religious authorities very firmly where they got off, and how they had brought the cause of liberty, " to ridiculous frustration " ; how, being mostly " vulgar bred up," they had behaved as such, and all had been greed, sequestrations, bribery, plurality, and persecution, and all under

cover of hypocritical zeal. Britain had never
been any good at governing, for " civility, prudence, love of the public good . . . are to this
soil in a manner outlandish ; grow not here, but
in minds well implanted with solid and elaborate
breeding." He puts this down to our lack of sun,
" which ripens wits as well as fruits." (It will
be observed that the historian did not hold with
Professor Freeman's view of the extermination of
British inhabitants, but traced an unbroken
descent from ancient to contemporary British
knaves and vulgars – unless indeed he attributed
the resemblance wholly to the unfortunate climate
they shared.) In any case, here is a sad fall from
the noble Britons, God's Englishmen, who had
figured so impressively in earlier pamphlets.
Milton knew now, and was seldom to forget, that
his countrymen were in the main deficient in wits
and frail in virtue. Only once or twice in future
was he to become again fulsome in their praise.

Besides writing history, he was busy doing more
of the Psalms into metre, of which the less said
the better. It might have been hoped that this
exercise had been abandoned for ever at the age
of fifteen ; but it has frequently been observed to
be an insidious and recurrent vice.

Meanwhile, like other men, he was closely
observing the course of politics, and, like the army,
turning from monarchist to republican, pushed
by the tortuous and irritating behaviour of the
unfortunate monarch doubling and redoubling
for his liberty and life. That Milton just now was
fuller of politics than of poetry, is clear from his
sonnet to the victorious General Fairfax, hope-
fully exhorting him to clear the land of fraud,
avarice, and rapine. This is, however, a much

better poem than that on his deceased Christian
friend, Mrs. Catherine Thomason, written a year
and a half earlier.   The fact is that Milton's poetic
genius was an extremely thin trickle just now.   It
might have been hoped that these four years'
abstention from pamphleteering would empoet
him again ; but it was not so.   Public spirit, that
bane of good poetry, kept him close to earth, and
not now nor ever was he able to say again
" *humum vix tetigit pede*."

It was with his feet firmly planted on the now
republican soil of England, that he published,
in February 1649, a fortnight after the King's
execution, his first anti-monarchical utterance,
The Tenure of Kings and Magistrates.

CHAPTER VI

SERVANT OF THE STATE

The Tenure of Kings and Magistrates is a summing up of the position its author was now arrived at in respect of tyranny, monarchy, republicanism, and the punishment of kings ; it is, in brief, a bold endorsement of tyrannicide. It is a contemptuous, coldly reasoned, intellectually aristocratic kind of a pamphlet, but impassioned by its writer's old furious dislike of clergymen. Anglican or Presbyterian, Roman or Independent, a minister of religion was to our author an incitement to a furious and bull-like charge, horns down, tail lashing, nostrils breathing smoke and fire. Apart from this excess of misoclericism, however, *The Tenure* is a moderate and rational enough piece of work.

It pleased the new regicide Council of State so well that they offered the author the Secretaryship for Foreign Tongues. He relates, in the *Defensio Secunda*, how he had gratuitously bestowed his various services on church and state, looking (unlike other men) for no reward but a good conscience, when behold, the Council invited him to lend them his services in the department of foreign affairs. Phillips calls him " *Latin* Secretary to the Council of State," who scorned " to carry on their Affairs in the Wheedling, Lisping Jargon of the Cringing *French*." Milton thus found himself employed to do for the government what he had always done for himself, write letters in Latin.

Why he undertook it, whether solely from public spirit, or partly for financial reasons, or from his natural liking for corresponding with eminent foreigners, or from desire to spend part of his day in work that took him out of his home, or from that subconscious desire to be employed on some work not creative which often attacks authors undecided as to their next invention, and perhaps still unripe for it, there is no knowing. Interesting though his work may have been, it is something of a downcome from that cry of hope of eight years before – " Then amidst the Hymns and Halleluiahs of Saints some one may perhaps bee heard offering in new and lofty Measures to sing and celebrate thy marvelous Judgements. . . ." Some one, at this time, was actually chiefly heard translating letters from foreign rulers into English and replies to them into Latin. And also reporting on the contents of pamphlets and papers submitted to him, with a view to censorship – an ungrateful task, one should suppose, to the author of *Areopagitica*.

He had also to write pamphlets on those persons and events which seemed to call for them, such as Ormond's *Articles of Peace with the Irish Rebels*, and *Eikon Basilike*. The Latin Secretary dealt faithfully in March with Lord Ormond, the Articles, the bloody Rebels and Papists of South Ireland, and the Presbyters " so haughtie in the Pontificall See of Belfast." In fact, no one comes well out of this pamphlet but Cromwell, who gets a fine resounding eulogy.

In October *Eikon Basilike* had to be answered
GM

with *Eikonoklastes*, which wears rather the air of a pamphlet written to order. It opens with the admission that " to descant on the misfortunes of a person fall'n from so high a dignity, who hath also payd his final debt both to Nature and his Faults," is not commendable. However, there is no further chivalry in the pamphlet. It is a dreary repartee to a dreary book, a recapitulation of the long tale of poor Charles's sins, interspersed with sharp reproofs of those who " are ready to give adoration to the Image and Memory of this Man, who hath offer'd at more cunning fetches to undermine our Liberties and putt Tyranny into an Art, then any British King before him."

Meanwhile, his sight was steadily deteriorating. What finally ruined it was the writing, through 1650, of the *Defensio Pro Populo Anglicano*, the answer he was ordered to make to the book by the celebrated foreigner Salmasius against the Commonwealth. Milton made a great business of his reply. He wrote it, as he says, in poor health, with failing eyes, and small leisure ; and he regarded it as " a far from despicable service to the valiant liberators of my country." It is a thoroughly bad performance, rude and silly in personal abuse, and in defamation of poor Charles, who is compared to Nero, accused of vicious wantonness, and of poisoning his father. The comments on the eminent writer whom he was refuting are in what has been called Latin Billingsgate – a tongue in which he was by now highly proficient. It reads curiously like an angry effort to assert himself, to dominate by sheer hectoring a world which had so far paid small attention to him, and which he had not now time or mood to conquer by that great epic which seemed to be receding into the distance behind piles of Foreign Office papers. Mounting his favourite language like a rostrum, he sets out to the continent of Europe what manner of man was John Milton, employed by the new and glorious rulers of England to keep foreigners in order and defend the English. He drums himself up to a kind of frenzied intoxication with his own powers, his own possession of the truth and of elegant Latin, his foe's complete lack (so he says) of either. The Council were delighted with the work, and thanked him much. Salmasius was furious, his enemies maliciously pleased. The learned man went about calling the insolent English writer a schoolmaster and worse. Milton felt that at last his reputation was growing to something like its proper stature in Europe, particularly when his book was publicly burnt by the hangman in Paris. Poor Salmasius, " after a faint dying Reply, was glad," says Phillips, " to have recourse to Death, the remedy of Evils and ender of Controversies." As a matter of fact, he did not die for three years. Milton was not ashamed to boast that he died of depression caused by his own attack ; which was possibly the most unchivalrous taunt he ever flung at a foe, and is only rivalled by the gibes of Salmasius and his friends against his own blindness – " a puppy, once my pretty little man, now blear-eyed . . . having never had any mental vision, he has now lost his bodily sight."

Such were the agreeable manners of literary and political controversy. Latin enjoys a tradition of scurrility above any other tongue, and the most violent abuse has always been written in it. Milton's familiarity with this tradition may account for much of his strong language, even when reviling in English.

Soon after the splenetic and prolonged splutter so grandly called the Defence of the English People, blindness fell on its author. He put it down himself to his faithfulness to this horrid book. " The choice lay before me between dereliction of a supreme duty and loss of sight . . . I decided to employ my little remaining sight in doing this, the greatest service to the common weal it was in my power to render." Thus he judged it, or perhaps chose to judge ; for if this work, on which his last light was spent, were not worth the sacrifice, his tragedy of darkness must have been unconsoled.

Added to it was the tragedy of the death of his infant only son. His wife, after supplying him with another child of the less perfect sex, died in June, 1652. We shall never know whether or not she and her husband had enjoyed any " conjugal sociability." Her best epitaph is Milton's own remark in the Divorce treatise –
" That every woman is meet for every man, none so absurd as to affirm." And that very few women were meet for John Milton, one may with safety add.

The *Defensio* had brought its author some international notoriety and visits from eminent foreigners. " He enters readily into talk," wrote one of these. " Of the old English theologians . . . he seemed to entertain an altogether too harsh, if not an unjust, opinion."

Meanwhile his blindness increased ; by March or April 1652, it was almost complete, and an assistant Latin Secretary had to be appointed. But Milton felt able, in May, to compose a sonnet, laudatory but exhortatory, " To the Lord Generall Cromwell, on the proposalls of certaine ministers at the Committee for Propagation of the Gospell." The ministers' proposals were concerned with the further limitation of religious freedom, and Milton broke out on the subject of " free conscience" and "hireling wolves" to Cromwell, the great champion of toleration, who " had rather Mahometanism were permitted among us than that one of God's children should be persecuted."

The sonnet to the younger Vane, written a month or so later, is less impassioned. Vane was another tolerationist : " the great shot of Cromwell and Vane," wrote Baillie, the Presbyterian recorder of the Westminster Assembly, " is to have a liberty for all religions without any exception." At any threats to liberty, " John Milton, a libertine that thinketh his wife a manacle and his very garters to be shackles and fetters to him, one that, after the Independent fashion, will be tied by no obligation to God or man," could be trusted to be up in arms, whatever his bodily or mental depression.

The same July there shot from the Hague the anonymous *Regii Sanguinis Clamor ad Coelum adversus Parricidos Anglicanos*. It dealt, in Latin as violent as Milton's own, with the virtues and learning of the great Salmasius, the crimes of the English Parricides against King, Church, People, and God, and the mean origin and vices of John Milton, a worm from the dunghill, a starving little grammarian, who had been expelled from Cambridge for his profligacy, and had fled to Italy from the disgrace, a hellish gallows-bird, a running rabbit, meaner than an ape, less than a louse. Rumour reported this to be by the well-known

French-Scottish theologian and preacher, Alexander More. Milton was commissioned to reply to this onslaught on his country, but did not at once do so ; he was in bad health, and blind, and was preparing for the expected attack of Salmasius himself. So he delayed his reply to the *Regii Sanguinis Clamor*, and meanwhile let his nephew, John Phillips, now a youth of about twenty, write a retort to an ill-written anonymous attack on himself of the year before. Young Phillips, his Latin supervised and emended by his uncle, " acquitted himself " says Anthony Wood, " very expertly in the art of raillery and giving imbittered language."

Salmasius, reported to be preparing another furious and slanderous onslaught on his enemy, died before it was finished. But Milton continued the battle, publishing his *Defensio Secunda* in the spring of 1654. The eulogistic passages addressed to Cromwell in this are tempered by decidedly worried admonitions, cautions and exhortations, the great man having by now assumed a virtual dictatorship.

The *Second Defence* is the most remarkable of Milton's Latin prose works. A magnificent medley, it begins with large boasts about himself, his countrymen, and the great times in which it had pleased God to cast them, that they might (respectively) perform and commemorate the noblest deeds since the foundation of the world. This extravagant praise of his fellow-citizens one suspects to be applied to only a small part of these at other times impatiently viewed beings – the noble band of regicides who had the government in hand. The others are " the misguided multitude," the same who were to be stigmatised in

Paradise Regain'd, by their Saviour, as "a miscellaneous rabble, who extol things vulgar." But
Milton was not here so outspoken, nor yet
so disillusioned, as this, though it is apparent
that he has, like the new Protector, pretty well
seen through parliamentary government and
elections.

From the nobility of the cause, he passes to his
own. He speaks, he says, without arrogance ;
this statement need be given no more weight than
his declared intention of not insulting Salmasius
after his death, or his remark that he is not
offended with More ; they are the common form
of all ages. But, in his platform view of Europeans,
waiting on his words with eager applause, while
he brings home to them the exile liberty, there
sounds the familiar note of self-intoxicated delu-
sion of grandeur. If I am he, he says, who laid
low in single combat the redoubtable Salmasius,
I shall speak now as one not unknown. Though
Salmasius has been laid low, his conqueror proceeds to trample on his corpse, before passing on
to the goring of Alexander More. These performances, like those of a triumphant but still angry
bull avenging itself for the banderillero's darts,
and the more self-exalting autobiographical
passages, should not, in fairness, be read or
quoted except side by side with the attacks which
occasioned them. When Milton boasts of the high
esteem in which he is, or has been, held, it has to
be remembered that he is clearing himself of
charges of vice. If his own statements, defensive
and offensive, are often in outrageous taste, so were
those which evoked them. He vaunts his personal
appearance because he has been called by his foes
a deformed monster, his Cambridge career when

accused of expulsion for profligacy, his blindness (a token of divine favour that should render him sacred from attack) in reply to cruel taunts on it. Not that this excuse holds for his angry raking up, with cries of execration, of More's goings on with servant maids, which seem to have provided such interesting gossip to his learned acquaintances.

But to this unchastened temper we owe, besides these scurrilities, the interesting passages of auto-biography in the *Defence*. Characteristically, they begin, " Who and whence I am, say you, is doubtful. So also was it doubtful who Homer was, who Demosthenes. . . ." He then outlines his life and work in the manner familiar to us. From this he passes to praises of the republic, attacks on the " tithe-pampered " Presbyterian clergy, and eulogy of Cromwell, ardent but not subservient. The Lord Protector is gravely admonished of the perilous pitfalls yawning on either side of the strait path he should tread, into some of which he has already fallen. There was no harm in the Protectorate ; rule by a great man, assisted by a Council of other great men is the ideal system, and better than the corruptions and follies of parliaments. But liberty there must be. If the very patron of liberty should at last offer violence to her whom he has defended, this slays all virtue. Keep, then, the right counsellors (he mentions several, who were in danger of losing favour). Next, leave the church to the church. (Cromwell had endorsed the decision of the Rump, " that the Magistrate hath power in mat-ters of Religion " ; he favoured hireling wolves, alias a state-paid ministry, and had established one commission to examine the fitness of new wolves and another to eject old ones.) And do not multiply laws (a great number had recently been passed), nor forbid things that should be free. Next, see to education, and reserve its rewards for the intelligent. Then, permit freedom of philosophy ; let all publish without censorship ; let not knowledge be meted out to us through the half-educated. Lastly, fear not to listen to anything, true or false, but listen least to those who would restrain freedom.

The mention of freedom leads him to a splendid exordium on its nature. Its burden is that of Sir Thomas Browne's exhortations on liberty, and, indeed, of many before him – that it begins at home, that civil freedom cannot be unless each man is his own conqueror. Unless he can expel from his thoughts superstition, avarice, ambition and luxury, " the tyrant whom you thought was to be sought abroad and in battle, you will find within, or rather many tyrants, daily engendered in your hearts. If you are not the victors here, that enemy whom you have conquered in battle is conquered in vain." Parliamentary corruption, lusts, follies, hatred and greed, enslave beyond liberation, for " it does not suit, nor fall to the lot of such men, to be free."

He might well have ended on this ; but he must mention again the services he has rendered to his country. " As for myself, to whatever state things may return, I have performed my work. . . ." Ominous words, which indicate the dark forebodings that he could not suppress. He sounds this note again – " If, after such brave achievements, you shall default, posterity shall thus pronounce judgment : The foundation was strongly laid . . . but men were wanting. Yet there was not wanting one to exhort, and encourage, and to celebrate the great deeds and their doers in praises that would endure for all time."

With this characteristic expectation, which seems the fulfilment of that other exalted prophecy of twelve years before, "One shall be heard . . ." the *Defensio Secunda* closes. It is Milton at his extraordinary best and worst, splendid, exasperating, scurrilous, moving, repulsive, and grandiose by turns. In nothing else he wrote is his passion for liberty so uncompromisingly shown ; it was become the chief end of life to him, and dark suspicions moved in him that it was to be betrayed after all. First the bishops ; then the Presbyterians ; and now even the Chief of Men, – all were for a state church, for paid preachers, for authority over religion. Liberty of worship, liberty of the press, liberty of marriage-dissolution – all these things tarried, and their apostle was slowly losing hope for the stupid, barbarous world which he exhorted in vain.

The *Second Defence* produced the sensation for which its author had hoped. Poor More moved heaven and earth, before its publication, to convince Milton that he was not the author of the *Regii Sanguinis*, and to get the *Defence* suppressed or altered ; and when it came over to Holland, he tried to buy it all up. He published a reply, as voluminously tagged with testimonials from eminent persons to his own character and learning as a book in a publisher's advertisement.

Milton replied to this with *Pro Se Defensio*, a tedious and discreditable piece of invective, in which he brings a number of fresh accusations against More's character, and defends his own, including his use of "language." "Who speaks of you, must speak obscenely," he rudely remarks.

This was the last shot in the Milton-Salmasius-Morus war. Indeed, even Milton's sense of the importance of showing these enemies up must have been somewhat dimmed by the horrid massacre of the Piedmontese Protestants that May, about which the Protector and Council and the Latin Secretary Extraordinary wrote letters throughout the summer, and the latter his famous (but not very good) sonnet on the subject.

About this time his salary was made a life-pension. He was, in fact, half retired, and had consequently more leisure for his own work.

CHAPTER VII

BLINDNESS

A NEW and quieter period for our author now began, in his house in Petty France. "So that being now quiet from State Adversaries and publick Contests," says Phillips, "he had leisure again for his own studies and private designs. . . . But the heighth of his Noble Fancy and Invention began now to be seriously and mainly imployed in a Subject worthy of such a Muse, *viz.* – A Heroick Poem, Entituled *Paradise Lost*. . . ."

He had by this time accepted his blindness as probably final, though he did not cease to try remedies. A tragic mood of despair, desperately trying for submission, is expressed in the sonnet,

> *When I consider how my light is spent,*
> *E'er half my days, in this dark world and wide,*

possibly written when his total blindness was a new and hideous fact. Very different in mood, and probably later, are the gay holiday sonnet to his young friend Lawrence, consulting him as to where they shall spend a day and dine together, and that to Cyriack Skinner on the same theme. His other sonnet to young Skinner is about his blindness, but serene ; he does not

> *bate a jot*
> *Of heart or hope ; but still bear up and steer*

Right onward.   What supports me, dost thou ask ?
The conscience, Friend, to have lost them overply'd
In libertyes defence, my noble task,
Of which all Europe talks from side to side.

He had here come to terms with life, or bravely
pretended to have done so. He was not, after
all, hiding his talent ; not only standing and
waiting. He was working ; though to what
extent this work was damaged by its hampering
conditions can never be known. But he reaped
now the reward of his long years of scholarly reading, and brought to his darkness a mind stored
with its rich miscellaneous fruits. He was read
to for several hours each day ; and his imagination, illumined, he says, by darkness, could work
on what his brain had stored. He was not, so
far as we can gather, unhappy in these years. He
had many friends, and some Continental reputation – not, no doubt, quite so much as he supposed, for that would scarcely have been possible ;
but " he was visited much by learned ; more than
he did desire," says Aubrey. " The only induce-
ment of severall foraigners that came over into
England was, chiefly to see O. Protector and
Mr. J. Milton, and would see the house and
chamber wher he was borne : he was much more
admired abrode than at home."

But he had also at home admiring friends.
Testimonies on the subject make him out to
have been good company – not only learned and
cultivated, but affable, and with a sharp wit ;
and the records of his Italian tour and his gay and
affectionate relations with young Lawrence and
Skinner bear this out. He had, of course, bitter
enemies, and, among some of the general public,

a vaguely sinister reputation. Here is the view of
an old Royalist lady in 1653 – " If I be not
mistaken, that is he that has wrote a book of the
Lawfulness of Divorce, and if report says true, he
had at that time two or three wives living. . . .
For the book that he wrote against the late King
that you would have me read, you should have
taken notice of God's judgment upon him, who
struck him with blindness. . . . "

But there were other ladies and gentlemen, of
different political colour, who sought his company.
The London of the middle fifties had once more a
cultivated society. It was recovering, under the
healing hand of time and the Protector's encouragement of letters and learning, its character as a
home of the Muses. There were music and poetry
and books, and civilised talk, though but for
Davenant's new opera house at the Cockpit, the
theatres remained barbarously closed. As for
company, Milton was, according to Phillips,
" frequently visited by persons of Quality, particularly my lady *Ranala*, whose son for some time
he instructed . . . and by particular Friends that
had a high esteem for him." Among these were
Marchmont Needham (the lively ex-editor of
Mercurius Politicus), Hartlib, Oldenburg, and
Durie, Andrew Marvell (who succeeded to the
Latin Secretaryship in 1657), young Lawrence,
and Cyriack Skinner. These last were both old
pupils of his, and Skinner, at least, was among
the many young men who acted sometimes as
amanuenses, as did also the Phillips nephews, now
picking up their living by casual literary jobs and
writing vulgar, facetious verse, and John anti-
Puritan satires. The Phillipses would be, no doubt,
so far as they frequented the Petty France circle,

lively elements in it.[1] The members of that
circle we hear least of were the three small
daughters, aged, when their mother died, six,
four, and about a month. Anne seems to have
been sickly and no good. Deborah (the most
like her father, says Aubrey, probably referring
only to appearance) proved, apparently, the
quickest and most apt to learn ; but what she
learned, how, and from whom, must remain vague.

In the autumn of 1656 their father presented
them with a stepmother, and himself with a new
wife, who seems, from his lines about her written
soon after her death, to have been all that he
could wish. He had at least been saved, this time,
from marrying on a face. But she died after
fifteen months, and again he was alone but for
his friends. The number of affable and interested,
though sometimes rather pompous and florid
letters (all in Latin) to friends, young and older,
English and foreign, which he wrote through this
time, testifies to his kindly, courteous and cheerful
relations with them. The misery of his blindness
only now and then breaks through ; and even
then it is usually balanced by references to his
brightened inward vision. " The light," he
writes to the French scholar, Elmeric Bigot, " is
not so much lost as turned inwards, for the
sharpening of my mind's edge. I do not renounce
books, badly as they have mulcted me, being
instructed against such peevishness by the example
of King Telephus of the Mysians, who did not
refuse to be cured by the weapon that had
wounded him." The weapon became, as he

---

[1] The interesting theory has been recently ably set forth by
Miss Helen Darbishire, in her *Early Lives of Milton*, that John
Phillips wrote the anonymous and pious Earliest Life.

grew used to wielding it in the new, hampered, sinister fashion, flexible and powerful in his hand.

Phillips told Aubrey that it was about two years before the King came in that the writing of *Paradise Lost* was actually begun. The drama had become an epic ; partly, perhaps, because plays were not now performable, more because of the advantages of narrative and description to the splendid, fantastic theme of a vast primeval Ptolemaic universe. It is less what the speakers say than what Milton says of them and their strange, dream-like, monstrous circumstances, that fascinates us in *Paradise Lost*. He has created a wild, transcendental, breath-taking universe, which is infinitely more alluring than any of its celestial or earthly denizens.

Meanwhile, he was at work on *De Doctrina Christiana*.

The *De Doctrina*, which was not printed until 1825, is a long account of what Milton had decided to be the body of Christian theology. Its contents were found, by some of the poet's early nineteenth-century admirers, a little odd. Here was this great, supposedly Puritan writer, laying down the law on theology and conduct with the superb individualism which might be expected by anyone who knew what to expect. He exalts Scripture, indeed, and bases his whole structure on what he believes it to say. But his use of it is yet one more example of the adaptability of the Scriptures to the needs of those who search them. As others have, Milton found that they spoke to him as he wished. Indeed, they never let him down. But above them (since the written word is liable to error) he exalts human reason, and the Spirit that enlightens men (intelligent men such as himself, one takes him to mean). The Christian miracles he treats rather cavalierly, as superfluous and slightly in the way ; while how literally he believed the Book of Genesis, of which he wove so superb a fantasy, we shall never know. He shows himself an Arminian, with a strong belief in the importance of man's free choice ; an Arian, maintaining that the Son is neither Co-essential nor Co-eternal with the Father, and that the Holy Ghost is less still ; and a (theoretic) polygynist, though a fervent misopolyandrist. He also comes out as a spirited anti-Sabbatarian ; as he truly remarks, the keeping of Saturday was commanded only to the Jews, and nothing ever said about transferring it to any other day, so why Sunday ?

The second book of the treatise deals with ethics, and is remarkable for the great variety of texts cited to recommend opposite lines of behaviour. There are some pleasant definitions, as, " Veracity consists in speaking the truth to those entitled to hear it," followed by an intelligent dissertation on those occasions and persons for which the truth is unsuitable. A due regard is shown for the virtues of courtesy, urbanity, and elegance of life and conversation, which recalls the *comis, affabilis*, of his admirer Isaac Vossius.

He seems to have been attached to no church, in either worship or doctrine. He was, indeed, as Dr. Johnson said, " predisposed . . . to such unbounded freedom as can hardly consist with any established system of faith whatever." He explains how important is the liberty of sifting every doctrine according to our individual persuasion. " Without this liberty we are still enslaved . . . under a barbarous tyranny."

Hм

But, since they assuredly *were* still enslaved, and particularly from 1660 on, he had the wisdom never to publish his siftings.

From such labours he roused himself, early in 1659, to address two new tracts to Richard Cromwell's first parliament. The first protests " that it is not lawfull for any power on Earth to compell in Matters of Religion," and is a spirited protest against the compelling of conscience and worship, which persecution is to be condemned more in the protestant than in the papist, as being contrary to his principle. As regards freedom of worship, he makes a regrettable exception – Roman Catholicism is not to be tolerated in England, " for reasons of state," for it is a foreign civil power, trying to keep up its dominion – the old English ground for persecution of Papists, who had always been punished as traitors, not as heretics. As to heresy, this Greek word should be explained to the people as meaning merely the following of any opinion, good or bad, in religion or other learning, as " after the exactest heresie of our religion I lived a Pharisee." Above all, there should be no state church.

But his protests had no effect. The established church was not disturbed by the new Protector's parliament, with its large anti-Republican majority. It had other matters than religious to trouble it. It died, and so did the new Protectorate, in May, and the old Rump and Council resumed the government. Milton, like the Vicar of Bray, retained his post through these vicissitudes of the British constitution. Indeed, now that the old Republicans were back in office, he felt more at home, more hopeful for his pet ideals, church disestablishment and religious liberty.

In August he published *The likeliest means to remove hirelings out of the Church*. After his usual custom (was not urbanity among the Christian virtues ?) he praises the new régime and adverts less favourably on the Protectorate. He then gets down to the hirelings, who were best not paid at all, but, since few would work gratis, and since the labourer is (he reluctantly supposes) worthy of his hire, they might receive voluntary offerings. But it were better that the clergy be brought up " to a competence of learning and to an honest trade," and so keep themselves, like St. Paul. Our clergy scarcely deserve public maintenance ; they are usually bad scholars and worse ministers, most of them were, when at the University, poor and pitiful boys of no promise. In brief, let Christendom rid herself of all her hireling crew and be happy.

But the restored Republicans abolished neither the state church nor tithes. Indeed, they scarcely would have had time to do so, had they desired, so speedily were they abolished themselves by Lambert's soldiers. Milton expressed himself on this high-handed *coup d'état* – " most illegal and scandalous, I fear me barbarous, that a paid army should . . . thus subdue the Supreme Power that set them up." Still, parliament had been weak on liberty of conscience and a state church, so was perhaps . . . " well dissolv'd." The Army must now choose a Council of State, whether an annual democracy or a perpetual aristocracy mattered little, in the face of " our Common Enemy, gaping at present to devour us." The Common Enemy was the Single Person

government which, in one form or another, was a
perpetual threat.

It was soon to be realised. When Monk
marched into London, and restored the old Long
Parliament with himself as virtual Dictator, and the
promise of a new "free Parliament," which would
inevitably be a Royalist parliament, and the City
roasted the Rump through a joyful night, Milton,
the rear-guard of the old Republicans, fighting to
the end, fired off his last pamphlet. He desired
" a General Councel of ablest men chosen by the
people " – a contradiction in terms, as he had
long since realised, but the hopeful phrase still
springs up, though the people, far from choosing
ablest men, were drifting like foolish slaves back
towards the captivity of kingship. His chosen
council, however, is at least not to be exposed
often to the whims of the electorate ; " being well
chosen, it should be perpetual." If Milton trusted
not the " single person," neither did he trust the
multitude. His forebodings of their ruin have a
melancholy as of an unheeded Cassandra.

" Where is the goodly tower of a Commonwealth, which the English boasted they would
build to overshadow kings, and be another
Rome in the west ? . . . If we return to Kingship, and . . . finde the old encroachments
coming on by little and little . . . which must
necessarily proceed from king and Bishop united,
we may be forc'd perhaps to fight over again
all that we have fought. . . . Considering these
things so plane, so rational. . . ."

But alas, few considered them. In vain their
defeated prophet exhorted " this torrent of the
people not to be so impetuos . . . to stay these
ruinous proceedings ; justly and timely fearing

to what a precipice of destruction the deluge of this epidemic madness would hurrie us " – all which eloquence was of no avail but to delight our ears again with a resurrection of the old cadenced eloquence which had so sadly languished of late. The *Readie and Easie Way to Establish a Free Commonwealth* makes fine bold reading, but its only effect was to annoy a parliament and public now resolved on monarchy. Milton was, not unnaturally, outed at last from his Secretary-ship. The Good Old Cause lay dead ; the Commonwealth perished in a blaze of bonfires and a fanfare of cannon ; King Charles was on the way ; and all was bustle, excitement and expense. Republicans could but flee or hide. Milton sought refuge with a friend in Bartholo-mew Close, a defeated and imperilled man, his cause and his world shattered in ruins about his ears.

CHAPTER VIII

PARADISE LOST

MILTON lay hid for about four months, until the Act of Indemnity, which surprisingly included him. His danger was great enough through this summer, so busy with plans for the vindication of outraged royalty. The Republican pamphleteer had every excuse for Tyburn or imprisonment for life except that of actual complicity in the royal execution. His old enemy, Prynne, a zealous worker in the cause of punishment, got him put on the long list of exceptions from indemnity ; he was ordered into custody, and two of his books were to be burnt. But, through the good offices of friends, he escaped the final black list.

That savage and bloody autumn passed, and Milton was among the living, and free by December to take a new house, where he resumed life and his epic of the Fall in the new, monarchised, prelatised, persecuting London of the Restoration, moving bitterly among the shattered fragments of a Republican poet's dream. Richardson records that he lived in perpetual terror of assassination, and that " He was so dejected he would lie awake whole nights " ; but adds, "Well it was for him that he had so fine an amusement, and a mind stor'd with rich ideas of the sublimest kinds " – well for him, in short, that he could now occupy himself with *Paradise Lost*, that most suitable theme

for contemplation in a lost and mad world, a
world in which it must have seemed to him that
all liberty, secular and religious, had gone under.
The hanging and quartering of his friends, the
disinterring of the dead regicides, one repressive
Act after another passed by the Cavalier Parliament, the formidable nets thrown about the Non-
conformists, the fettering of the press, the power
of the bishops, here was a return into Egypt indeed, for the bitter misoclere, for the proud
libertarian whose very garters were shackles to
him, for the Republican to whom the Single
Person was anathema.

There remained his work. He threw himself
ardently into the continuation of *Paradise Lost*.

Of his life in Jewin Street, with his three young
daughters, whom he apparently tried to train to
be of service to him, several accounts remain.
The girls, ill-taught children as they had been,
did not, it seems, take kindly to languages or
reading aloud ; they were definitely not, as their
cousin Edward Phillips remarks, inheritrixes of
their father's learning ; they were irked " almost
beyond endurance," and showed it. The eldest,
Anne, by that beneficent working of the subconscious self which does so much for us all, had, it
seems, early induced some impediment in her
speech, which excused her. Mary and Deborah
had not thought of this, and had to go through
it. The well-known story of their having to read
uncomprehended languages aloud seems rather
tall ; but doubtless they suffered, and " broke
out more and more," says their cousin Edward,
" into expressions of uneasiness." Ill-regulated
girls, as they grew older, they sold their father's
books to the dung-hill woman, and helped the

maid to cheat him over the marketing ; or so
said the gossiping tongues of servants and stepmother after his death.

It can scarcely have been a happy family life,
in spite of its patriarch being " the life of the conversation " ; but the girls may not actually have
suffered greatly, since their father was apparently
surrounded by willing assistants, and " kept a
man to read to him," and they themselves were
presently sent out to learn embroidery. Deborah,
at least, used to say in later life that her father
had been delightful company ; she had forgiven,
and no doubt forgotten, the Hebrew and Greek,
if any. She had, perhaps, even forgiven being
rung for in the night, " at what hour whatsoever,"
to take down the lines that her father had just
composed.

Elizabeth Minshull, the young woman who
became the third Mrs. Milton in 1663, does not
appear to have been troubled in this way. She
had been recommended to Milton as a good wife
who would make him comfortable, but she
appears to have been firm as to rendering no
secretarial assistance. As to her character, it
varies, like most characters, on different tongues.
Aubrey called her " a gent. person, a peacefull
and agreeable humour." Richardson had heard
she was a Termagant, and hard on her step-
daughters. We know that she wrangled un-
generously about her husband's will. But she
provided him with dishes that he liked, and it is
possible that, for the rest, he did not greatly
observe her. The years were long since gone in
which he would passionately weigh the merits of
his wife as a companion and call heaven and earth
and the decalogue to witness that his life was, on

her account, a cohabiting desolation. He had more important things to think about, now that he was engaged on his tremendous epic of heaven, earth and hell.

In a book of small compass one scarcely dares to comment on *Paradise Lost* ; such an occupation would, if given its head, fill a large volume, and, indeed, has extremely often done so. The fascinations of this huge, baroque, classic, romantic, Catholic, Protestant, devil-haunted, learned, amusing, derivative, unique fairy-tale, are inexhaustible. The scheme has been treated variously down the ages, by Orientals, Greek and Latin Christians, Anglo-Saxon poets, Swedes, Italians, Dutchmen, and who not. Cynewulf has that same desolate, wind-stormed chaos, Caedmon that loveliness of flower and emerald sward and a most appealing Eve, Andreini and Grotius a noble Adam, Du Bartas a most painstaking week of Creation. Common to literature in this kind are the wily serpent, the bustling, skirmishing, good and bad angels, the capricious and somewhat unreasonable Almighty presiding over a Ptolemaic universe of spheres within spheres. But no other writer has built up the tremendous structure which Milton saw against the darkness, and to which he gave such magnificent, unearthly life, peopling it with the creatures which his imagination threw up, to stalk the universe much larger than life. And, leavening and colouring the whole splendid mass of thought, theology and fancy projected by this our greatest subjectivist, is his own life's experience. Nothing that was Milton, nothing that had happened to Milton, throughout his dreaming, passionate and disillusioning life, but is to be found in *Paradise*

Lost. First the imaginative child, poring over Sylvester, assimilating phrases that were to pour themselves into his epic half a century later. Then the boy, at school and Cambridge, amassing classical lore, which rises aptly or inaptly to his lips at every turn, whenever simile or allusion can be intruded. Then the lover; the same dart that had pierced the youth descrying a fair face pierces our great progenitor when he observes his new and female playmate. And all the excited passion of *In adventum veris* is in the amorous groves and nuptial bowers of Eden, when

> . . . *fresh Gales and gentle Aires*
> *Whisper'd it to the Woods, and from thir wings*
> *Flung Rose, flung Odours from the spicie Shrub,*
> *Disporting, till the amorous Bird of Night*
> *Sung Spousal, and bid haste the Evening Starr.*

This is the cry of spring which the boy of twenty had uttered, when Earth had poured forth spices and roses and cried *Io Hymen!* That vernal ecstasy is evoked again

> . . . *while Universal* Pan
> *Knit with the* Graces *and the* Hours *in dance*
> *Led on th' Eternal Spring.*

The country loveliness of Horton is here, with its lawns and level downs and grazing flocks, and the " Woodie Theatre " seems set for a performance of *Arcades* or *Comus.* Sometimes the English landskip breaks into the Italian, with its " mantling vine," and Vallombrosa brooks. Or else Eden becomes an unvisited but imagined Grecian or Assyrian land, rich and odorous with amiable delicious trees.

Milton has been charged with not being a realistic nature-observer ; his answer might be, what did he want with actual nature, when he could imagine a garden of such luxuriant curious loveliness of detail, such steep magnificence of design ?

After Italy, the anti-prelatic pamphlets. Here the Archangel Michael is quite explicit, freely mentioning the faults of clergymen, their superstitions, lucre and ambition, and the other ecclesiastical points on which he found himself in such close agreement with Milton and instructed our first sire.

The reflection of our poet's next important experience, his first marriage, is obvious ; for the tale of Eden centres round the disastrous victory of sensual folly over reason. Adam (like Milton when he was teaching small boys) felt that he would like a companion, he was tired of being alone among the animals ; though he had only had three days of it, it seemed, and indeed was, a life-time. Seeing the lovely Eve, he is enraptured. She seems all that is most admirable, and is led blushing to the nuptial bower. Raphael takes him severely to task about his too carnal conception of love –

> *What higher in her societie thou findst*
> *Attractive, human, rational, love still ;*
> *In loving thou dost well, in passion not,*
> *Wherein true Love consists not.*

Adam's love-story is happier than his creator's, for his Eve was, until she ingorged the downy fruit (apparently a peach), all that he could have wished in a wife – more like the too transient

Katharine Woodcock than poor Mary Powell, in
"those thousand decencies" which indicated union
of mind. She spoke, too, very properly, pointing
out that she enjoyed far the happier lot, having a
consort so greatly superior to his, even if she was,
as she thought, rather the nicer-looking. At
which our first Father,

> *Smil'd with superior Love . . .*
> *. . . and press'd her Matron lip*
> *With kisses pure.*

It was, in fact, at first a thoroughly happy
marriage ; and it was not until the affair of the
fruit that passion dragged our general ancestor
to his destruction, as marriage with the unsuitable
girl, Mary, dragged his descendant. It was after
the Fall that Adam deplored woman and gave
his views on marriage, putting into verse passages
from the divorce tracts, and bewailing the " dis-
turbances on Earth through Female snares."
However, Eve, seeking pardon, was partially
forgiven, even as Mary had been ; though her
spouse's words do not appear to offer hope for a
much happier conjugal life in the future than was
enjoyed by the ill-matched inheritors of his woe.
Adam looked forward to

> *A long days dying to augment our paine,*
> *And to our Seed (O hapless Seed !) deriv'd.*

The heart had gone out of his love and his life ;
he was cast from Paradise, on to the hard, disillusioning, and barren earth, on which, after
rejecting the alternative suggestions put forward
by the unbalanced Eve of birth control or suicide,
he resigns himself to live and procreate his hapless

seed. He is left with a deep scar of disillusionment
as to love, life, and women.

> *Thus it shall befall*
> *Him who to worth in Women overtrusting*
> *Lets her Will rule ; restraint she will not brook.*

Personal liberty thus having been forfeited
through enslavement to passion, Milton had fore-
seen, and Michael tells Adam, that public liberty
too will fail. " One shall rise, of proud ambitious
heart," who shall domineer over his fellows.
Michael is a firm Republican, and knows that the
Single Person government will not do. He also
shares Milton's irritation with weakness of intellect.

> *O that men*
> *(Canst thou believe ?) should be so stupid grown.*

Th'archangel is, in fact, of Milton's political,
religious, and intellectual colour throughout, and
a firm adherent of the Good Old Cause. He
believes in Church Disestablishment and religious
toleration. He also feels that pessimism as to the
world's future, which, in Milton, succeeded the
first glorious faith in the revolution. It will " still
tend from bad to worse," until the Judgment
Day. Milton's hope for a new world had been
dying in bitterness for years before the return of
the monarchy hung, drew and quartered the
already dead Republic and swung its carcase on
a gibbet for the derision of a delighted nation,
amid " the barbarous dissonance of Bacchus and
his Revellers."

The poet's stormy egoism finds expression in
almost all the creatures of his imagined universe.

In turn he is the hectoring Almighty; the conjugal, loquacious, superior Adam; the informative, admonishing, chattering, heartily eating, amorous, passion-disapproving angel Raphael; the austerer Michael, coming to prophesy the truth about the world and to exact penalties; the rebellious Satan, who will brook no restraint. He is only, I think, not to be discerned in the feckless, erred, adoring Eve.

Space lacks to speak here of the theology, the philosophy, or the prosody, of *Paradise Lost*; of its literary form, its derivations, borrowings, and transmutations, its cosmography, its inconsistencies and anachronisms, its rich weight of lore and learning, the unintended humours of the lordly Adam and his amiable Eve, who longed at times to get on with her gardening without being talked to by her long-winded spouse. There can be no poem in any language in which bathos and beauty so jostle one another, and pedestrianism so alternates with wingy flights. It is by turn magnificent, engaging, tragic, tedious, fantastic, and entertaining; and has, throughout, the queer enchantment of the exotic, monstrous mind which shaped it.

CHAPTER IX

LAST YEARS

Paradise Lost was finished in 1665 ; and soon afterwards the Plague drove the Miltons from Artillery Walk to the Buckinghamshire village of Chalfont St. Giles. The Great Plague past, they returned to London well in time for the Great Fire, which burnt up Bread Street and the paternal house which provided part of Milton's income. He must have lived, during the Artillery Walk years, on straitened, but not incommodious means. His wife seems to have been a good manager, lovely in Adam's sense of the word, " for nothing lovelier can be found in woman than to studie household good." It seems most likely that she did not understand a word he wrote, or a thought he had, other than gastronomical. If we may judge from the bitter invective against practically all women and wives which runs through *Samson Agonistes*, presumably composed partly during his third wedded state, Milton had not bettered his views on the sex by familiarity with his latest spouse ; still he indicts this section of the human race with the misogynist fury of a Christian Father ; his

> . . . *anger, unappeasable, still rages,*
> *Eternal tempest never to be calm'd.*

Kept at least in physical comfort (in so far as

this is a possible condition for a man " tormented with headaches, gout, blindness") by his wife's ministrations, read to and written for by friends, daughters, hired man or other assistants of varying degrees of usefulness, Milton spent these dark, disappointing years in hard imaginative work, brightened by the companionship of friends.

In the two years between the finishing and the publication of *Paradise Lost*, he was, apparently, composing *Paradise Regain'd*. At what point he determined on this, whether it was really, as Mr. Thomas Ellwood improbably supposed, at the moment when this simple young man told Milton that he had not said anything in *Paradise Lost* about Paradise Found, or at some earlier or later time, history does not relate.

Christ's temptation in the wilderness was not a new theme in poetry ; Milton obviously had Giles Fletcher's *Christ's Victorie and Triumph* in his mind, and probably other temptation poems and dramas. But, despite this, and despite the Jobian structure, he makes of both theme and form something very characteristically his own. He keeps wholly to the desert episodes, the inner conflict, the colloquies of Satan with Christ and his consultations with his infernal peers as to what to try next, and panoramic views of the history and thought of the world. What he was concerned to expound was the godlike soul rejecting temptation and thus winning that liberty which cannot exist with slavery to passion. His Christ is his ideal man ; what he is certainly not is the Jesus of the Gospels. As has been pointed out[1] his classical education and contempt for the people (he calls them "a herd confus'd, a miscellaneous

[1] E. M. W. Tillyard, *Milton*.

rabble") sit oddly on him.   He has, too, a certain
Miltonic arrogance of spirit, and a decidedly
Miltonic and un-Christlike egoism, in, for instance, the long passage of soliloquy in which he
recalls, with what may almost be called smugness,
what a good, industrious, and serious childhood
had been his, and how, in the Temple, he had
been "admir'd by all."

There is, in this quiet epic in unimpassioned
dialogue, none of the pictorial lavishness of
Paradise Lost. It is a sober, reasoned business,
with a fiend of an altogether inferior order
(though redeemed by a commendable knowledge
of Greek philosophy and literature) to the Satan
who had defied God, and a few lines are incom-
parably flat, such as Christ's reply when the fiend
enquires how he does after the storm – "Me
worse than wet thou find'st not." But the whole
epic is firm and closely knit, and has the spiritual
force of sustained conflict.   Its interest centres in
Milton's recession upon the inner life of the soul,
all outer hope having failed him.   Eden is long
since lost ; it is a very different, and no external,
Eden, which is to be raised in the vast wilderness
of the defeated and melancholy world.

Paradise Lost was published in 1667, after some
trouble with the Reverend Thomas Tomkyns, the
licenser.   Milton made a fair contract with a
publisher for it ; it had not, probably, the air of a
best-seller ; though, as to that, compositions less
attractive-looking had proved to be so, the taste
of readers being then, as now, wholly unpredict-
able.   The sale at first was slow, and the reception
doubtful.   The subject was thought by many
readers either hackneyed or irreverent ; the treat-
ment was voted slow, and the blank verse form

Iᴍ

very strange. Richardson says that " it lay neglected for two or three years," and puts this down to party partiality and the then gay taste of wit. A year after its issue, the publisher got the poet to improve the volume by prose arguments describing each book, and a note on the verse, mentioning that Rime was the invention of a barbarous age to set off wretched matter and lame meter. This, or the steady force of percolation, sent up the sales. Dryden made his famous comment, " This man cuts us all out, and the ancients too." The prejudice against blank verse (" Why, Mr. Dryden," as a country gentleman justifiably enquired, " is it not in Rime ? ") no doubt was a handicap ; still, the book's reputation gained ground. The blind Republican pamphleteer won respect as a poet from many who abhorred his politics.

Encouraged by his increased popularity, Milton published a Latin Accidence in 1669, and his *History of Britain* the next year, after the licenser had amputated such comments as were considered (and doubtless intended) to reflect unfavourably on the present age. They are since restored, and add considerable spirit to the chronicle of our ancestors' foolish and barbarous doings.

In 1671 *Paradise Regain'd* was published, with *Samson Agonistes, A Dramatic Poem.* Samson had been in Milton's mind for a tragic drama since 1641 ; now that dramas were in fashion again, and now that Samson had become so tragically and variously identified with himself, it must have become a haunting theme. *Samson* is the least objective of the three great poems, the saddest, the most reminiscent of the polemical Milton, the angry, embittered, defeated Republican. Taken immediately from the Book of Judges, possibly, but not certainly, owing something to Vondel's contemporary drama on the same theme, derived in form and structure from classical tragedy, and particularly from Aeschylus, *Samson* derives in spirit and detail (allowing for the transmutation into art) directly from Milton's own experiences. It is, in fact, almost a crypto-autobiography and jeremiad on current affairs ; and not so crypto as to make its getting past the licenser seem anything but rather odd.

Samson laments, in what reads like one of the autobiographical passages from the pamphlets,

> *I was his nursling once and choice delight,*
> *His destin'd from the womb. . . .*
> *He led me on to mightiest deeds*
> *Above the nerve of mortal arm*
> *Against the uncircumcis'd, our enemies. . . .*

He had been the pride of his parents, once champion and darling of his countrymen ; but their servile minds had rejected their deliverer ; he is " betrayed, Captiv'd, and both my Eyes put out." There follows the cry of blinded desolation –

> *O dark, dark, dark, amid the blaze of noon,*
> *Irrecoverably dark, total Eclipse*
> *Without all hope of day ! . . .*
> *The Sun to me is dark*
> *And silent as the Moon,*
> *When she deserts the night*
> *Hid in her vacant interlunar cave. . . .*

He is more wretched than the vilest creature who can see ; he is exposed to daily fraud, contempt,

abuse, and wrong, in power of others, never in his
own. It is lament without hope, the anguish of a
proud and brave man under the unendurable.
He breaks out against God, who cheats men

> *With gifts and graces eminently adorn'd*
> *To some great work, thy glory,*
> *And peoples safety, which in part they effect,*

and then abandons them to degradation or " the
hostile sword," their carcases exposed, the prey of
dogs and fowls, or to " unjust tribunals, under
change of times," or else they live in poverty,
with painful diseases (such, doubtless, as gout)
which should be the punishment of dissolute days.
How agonisingly the torturing deaths of the
regicides haunted him is betrayed in the reference
to torment which preys on the spirit,

> *As on entrails, joints, and limbs,*
> *With answerable pains, but more intense.*

Then there is Delilah, the unsatisfactory wife
chosen from the enemy's ranks, the embodiment
of the treachery of her deplorable sex, in address-
ing whom Samson seems to hint that Mary
Powell, despite the reconcilement and her
" feign'd remorse," had been as annoying as ever
during her subsequent married life. The best men,
beguiled to forgive the penitent,

> *Are drawn to wear out miserable days.*
> *Entangl'd with a poysnous bosom snake.*

He tells Delilah (forgetting momentarily that he is
not a Greek and familiar with Circe) that her

" fair enchanted cup, and warbling charms " have
no power over him. She departs, and the interested Chorus pass disparaging remarks on women
and their love, and speculate on what it is that
makes them so worthless. They allude to the
veiled virgin familiar to us from the divorce tracts,
who, once married, proves " a cleaving mischief."

> *Therefore God's universal Law*
> *Gave to the man despotic power*
> *Over his female in due awe,*
> *Nor from that right to part an hour.*

And so Milton delivers his soul of one rankling
trouble after another, sublimating his bitterness,
finally releasing himself in that glorious wish-
fulfilment of the pulling of his enemies' city upon
their heads.

> *Lords, Ladies, Captains, Councellors, or Priests,*
> *Their choice nobility and flower . . .*
> *While their hearts were jocund and sublime,*
> *Drunk with Idolatry, drunk with Wine,*

the avenger descended on them as an evening
dragon, and bolted his cloudless thunder on their
heads. What a vengeance, what a reversal of
wrong ! " Ali is best," say the Chorus, and there
will now be, for God's servants, " calm of mind all
passion spent."
Was there ? Did the wreaking of his great
imaginary vengeance, and the sublimation of his
experience leave Milton calm, purge his bosom of
some of its perilous stuff ? It must, anyhow, have
soothed his assaulted pride. He was now a poet,
admired even by his enemies –

So vertue giv'n for lost,
Deprest, and overthrown, as seem'd,
Like that self-begott'n bird
In the Arabian *woods embost,*
That no second knows nor third,
Revives, reflourishes, then vigorous most
When most unactive deem'd,
And though her body die, her fame survives
A secular bird ages of lives.

Dramatically, *Samson Agonistes* is weakened by the fact that its grand climax, and only action, takes place " off," and is only revealed to us by the rather flat narration of a diffuse and wordy messenger with little dramatic sense. It is in its incidental splendid passages, and its emotional tensity, that its great beauty lies.

It was the last of Milton's great works. After it (in the same year, 1673, which saw also his new and enlarged Collected Poems) came a tract called *True Religion, Haeresie, Schism, Toleration, And what best means may be us'd against the growth of Popery,* occasioned by the King's Declaration of Indulgence of 1673, which so agitated the Protestant dovecotes, rousing again the terror of Roman Catholic predominance which had been burnt deeply into English nerves, and which made even Halifax, most rational and moderate of men, except this branch of the Christian tree from the toleration he advocated. Milton pleads for toleration for nearly all sects, but when he enquires " whether Popery be tolerable or no?" the answer is No. For Popery is political, its state activities are dangerous. Further, it is idolatrous ; and here is revealed Milton's hardening and narrowing since he wrote on this subject in 1659. His hatred of

Popery has been intensified by its growth at court and by suspicion of the King's secret aims, and probably too by his own embittering years. Popish worship, then, must be hindered in England, except, he adds, among foreigners. Not by punishment, for this would be against the clemency of the Gospel. But we must "remove their idolatry, and all the furniture thereof," he largely and vaguely says. Also, we should amend our lives, for where wickedness abounds Popery will grow apace, since the wicked, wrung by conscience and the peril of their souls, will, rather than go to the pains of amendment, fly to the offices of this church.

It was the last blast of the war trumpet of the veteran pamphleteer ; 1674, the last year of his life, was marked by a new edition of *Paradise Lost*, and by the publication of those of our author's Latin private letters of which he had kept copies, together with some of his Cambridge orations and exercises. Milton was by now grown famous enough for any scraps he had kept (and he was a great keeper of his own compositions) to be worth a publisher's while. The printer's hope had been to publish the Cromwellian state letters with the private correspondence, but official leave for these was naturally not granted, and Milton supplied some of his academic exercises, to make up the book. The result was a very agreeable and interesting volume. Without it there would be a whole side of Milton, and more especially of the young Milton, so pathetically and tragically like and unlike the old, in the absurd height of his ingenuous, dreaming pride, that we should scarcely know.

Turning over these young declamations, the

blind, defeated, now unhoping Republican, his
ardent illusions about human possibilities and his
own glorious future turned into nightmares that
mocked his darkness, into bitter dreams of some
enormous revenge, into a passionate, painful,
striving to believe that " all is best, though we oft
doubt," must have felt pity, half wistful, half
cynical, for that splendid, opinionated youth, so
avid for learning, so touching, so often absurd
(but perhaps this aspect of his youth was to Milton
the least obvious).   After all, in spite of slain
dreams, and the chasm that yawned between the
young man and the old, filled with political strife,
disillusionment, defeat, and " lot unfortunate in
nuptial choice," the two were the same man, one
might almost say the same adolescent ; stormy,
sensitive, arrogant, painfully egotistic, equally
far from that calm of mind, all passion spent,
which was the impossible aspiration of both.

The Letters and Prolusions appeared in the
July of 1674.   Their author died of the gout that
autumn, and had, says Edward Phillips, " a very
decent interment according to his Quality, in the
Church of St. Giles, Cripplegate."

He had committed the carelessness of dying in-
testate, or rather, with no written will, but his
widow, supported by Christopher Milton, who
acted for her, and the maidservant, declared that
he had, in conversation, some time back, directed
that all his property was to go to her, and that
" the unkind children " of his first wife were to
have only the marriage-portion still owed him
by their grandfather, " they having been very
undutiful to me."   Long legal wrangling failed
to prove this will, and the girls got a hundred
pounds apiece.

While these squabbles about his small estate occupied the attention of his family, such part of the literary world as admired him broke into eulogies of the " author of most deserved fame, late deceas't." Tended by Dryden and a few others, his fame grew, against all the detractions of the Rhymers. By the end of the century, it was secure, though still, in the eighteenth century, vastly and hugely to grow.

CHAPTER X

On Milton as a poet, his relation to his time, to his contemporaries and to the whole body of ancient and modern literature, his original contribution to poetry, his gift of blank verse to a surprised, protesting, but ultimately all too subserviently accepting nation, his prosody, his classical structure, his subject-matter – on all these comments have been made with varying degrees of intelligence, but without cease, for two centuries. Every conceivable parallel and derivation of everything he said, almost of every phrase he used, has been sought and found. More than most writers, he has suffered from charges of borrowing. Without going so far as to endorse his loyal widow's " Mr. Milton borrowed from none but his own Muse," we can relegate all this business of borrowing, conscious and unconscious, to the sphere of literary curiosity ; it is less a factor in our estimate of Milton than a testimony to his enormous reading. Every reminiscent phrase with which he mosaicked his work, became, hammered into shape on his anvil, his own possession, transmuted, as he transmuted the idiom which he caught from the ancients. " Milton's language," said Jonathan Richardson, " is English, but 'tis Milton's English ; 'tis Latin, 'tis Greek English ; not only the Words, the Phraseology, the Transpositions, but the Ancient Idiom is seen in all he writes, so that a Learned Foreigner will think Milton the Easiest to be understood of All the English Writers."

He was, in fact, an Ancient. An Ancient, and, in some sort, a Learned Foreigner himself; the least English, the most alien, of the English poets. One approaches him dubiously, as one approaches Dante or Michael Angelo, rather in fascinated surprise than in love, for here seems a phœnix, that self-begotten bird, that no second knows nor third, an exotic bird from afar, of brilliant plumage and strange cries. Grant that this is nonsense, that Milton was hatched on the nest of seventeenth-century England, bred by the Renaissance Elizabethans out of the Ancient World, nursed by Puritanism and fed by a thousand foods, ancient and modern, English and foreign, yet still he wheels and soars before our dazzled eyes, still seems a self-begott'n bird. Grant, too, that he had a thousand successors, a whole progeny of imitators; yet still he had no successor. Find in him Spenser and the Spenserians, Dante and the medievals, the Renaissance, the Elizabethans, Greece, Rome, Israel, and the land of the Chaldees; and still you have not explained Milton. He had a musical ear and training, a capacious brain, classical and much other erudition; he was a unique blend of Hellenism, Hebraism, Classicism, Romanticism, and Baroque; he read and wrote so much Latin that it bent and twisted his English into Roman knots and bows; he wrote much of his prose in such a temper that he could not finish his sentences; his invective he borrowed from the rudest medieval Latinists, his prose cadences from the very air of

his period, his allusions from the lore of every
land. His style, usually close-packed, is at times
flatly diffuse. He writes, with magnificent cere-
mony, of beings whose conversation moves us to
mirth, such as Adam and the angel Raphael.
Of humour he knew little except in its un-
amiable form of heavy and coarse sarcasm. Of
the varieties of human character he knew less ;
he saw people not in the round, but as types, or
else as projections of some experience or passion
in himself. His tremendous imagination pene-
trates chaos and the spheres, but never the human
soul, creates for us a universe, a glorious garden,
or the very desolation of human despair, but not
the subtler play of mind and heart. His verbal
dexterity is used to make beauty, to give us an
English renovated and richer, to pierce us with
intellectual and sensuous delight, but never as
a medium for that felicitous rapier play of mind
and speech that the dramatist of human beings
has at command. A comedy by Milton would be
a nightmare ; one imagines an attempted horrid
mixture of Aristophanes and Jonson. Masque,
epic, and tragedy, gave scope to his loveliness, his
numerous harmony, his stately soaring in heroic
realms ; but even here, his lack of power to
handle the delicate complexities of human nature
weakens him.

As a man he was, despite his disconcerting con-
tradictions, of a fundamental simplicity. He
possessed an undue share of sensitive, irritable and
vaunting egotism ; the portion of poets, but con-
cealed by some of them better than by this sub-
jective, almost humourless great man, who saw
himself as God's nursling, as his country's prophet, and at the last as a vanquished Titan ; and

always, conquering or conquered, in the right. Yet this view of himself he must have politely subdued in intercourse with friends, for his company was esteemed and found agreeable. "I never," said one of his biographers, "heard that he was by any called morose." And Aubrey – "Of a very cheerful humour. He would be cheerful even in his gout-fits, and sing."

Vix humum tetigit pede, he wrote of his soaring youth ; but by middle life he was struck down to earth. He died a vanquished and embittered idealist, in a world with which he had never come to terms, nor could.

BIBLIOGRAPHY

Milton's Complete Works, Verse and Prose (with translations). 19 vols. Columbia University Press.

Works in Verse and Prose, with Life. J. Mitford. 8 vols.

Poetical Works, with critical notes. W. Aldis Wright.

Poetical Works, after original text. H. C. Beeching.

Poems (arranged chronologically). H. J. C. Grierson. 2 vols.

Facsimile of Trinity MS. of Minor Poems. W. Aldis Wright.

Commonplace Book. A. J. Horwood. (Camden Society.)

Prose Works. English, Latin, and translations, with Letters and Academic Exercises. Charles Symmons. 7 vols.

Life of Milton and History of his Time. David Masson. 7 vols.

Early Lives of Milton, with Introduction. Helen Darbishire. (Contains the lives by Aubrey, the Anonymous Biographer, Wood, Edward Phillips, Toland, and Jonathan Richardson.)

Lives of Edward and John Phillips. William Godwin.

Milton. E. M. W. Tillyard.

Milton. Walter Raleigh.

Milton. Mark Pattison.

The Youth of Milton. J. H. Hanford.

Chronology of Milton's Private Studies. J. H. Hanford.

Milton's Sonnets : Smart